The Eugene V. Debs Reader:
Socialism and the Class Struggle

The Eugene V. Debs Reader: Socialism and the Class Struggle

Edited by
William A. Pelz

Introduction by
Howard Zinn

Institute of Working Class History
CHICAGO

The Eugene V. Debs Reader:
Socialism and the Class Struggle

Copyright-2000
Institute of Working Class History
First Printing: 1 May 2000

The right of William A. Pelz to be identified as the editor of this
work has been asserted by him in accordance with the Copyright,
Designs and Patents Act of 1988.

Published by:
Institute of Working Class History
2335 West Altgeld Street
Chicago, Illinois 60647-2001, U.|S.A.
e-mail: iwch@juno.com

European inquiries to:
BP5, Bxl 46
rue Wiertz
1047 Brussels, Belgium

Desktop publishing design, layout
and production by
Alynne Romo

Cover: Art Work by Carlos Cortez,
Member, Industrial Workers of the World, IU 450,
Printing and Publishing House Workers

ISBN: 0-9704669-0-0
Library of Congress Control Number: 00-92764

Printed in the USA by Morris Publishing
3212 East Highway 30
Kearney, NE 68847
1-800-650-7888

Acknowledgments

This volume would not have been possible without the contribution of numerous people. Among them is the famous IWW artist Carlos Cortez who took time out of his busy schedule to produce the original Debs woodblock which graces this book. Justly renowned historian, Howard Zinn added vital historical context with his clear and powerful introduction. Lauren Compton and Todd LaRue were both incredibly invaluable in setting down the words, proofreading the works, and helping with last minute production details.

Throughout the project, Eric Schuster was a source of constant encouragement and giver of sound advice. The work also profited by excellent and thought-provoking insights from Prof. Jie-Hyun Lim.

J. Quinn Brisben, Wendell Harris, David McReynolds, Kay Meyers, Greg Pason and Frank Zeidler continue to carry on the spirit of Debs and to fight for the socialist dream.

Countless others rendered advice and inspiration. Among the most notable were Alexander Pantsov, Mario Kessler, Caleb Jennings, Arthur S. Kazar and Theodore Bergmann.

Lastly, Engels, my cat, was always quick to insert himself into the project at every stage of development and was particularly keen on rearranging pages of the manuscript to better fit his own intellectual predilections. Of course, any editorial mistakes or production errors are his, not mine or any of the other people associated with this project.

—Dr. William A. Pelz, 1 May 2000

The Eugene V. Debs Reader: Socialism and the Class Struggle

Contents

Editors Preface

Note on selections:

It speaks to the power of Debs that so many disparate political currents have tried to stake claim to his legacy. Social Democrats, Communists[1], Liberals[2] and Trotskyists[3] have all sought to incorporate him into their tradition albeit with rationalizations for those occassions Debs deviated from their proscribed protocol. Many past volumes containing Debs writings and speeches bear the mark of such preoccupations. The current editor certainly makes no claim for any mythical objectivity as all humans are products of their time and place in history. Yet, an attempt has been made to allow Gene Debs speak for himself without attempting to "spin," excuse or reinterpret his words. Most of the following selections have been out of print for over half a century and thus inaccessible to many would-be readers.

Eugene Victor Debs (1855-1926)

Trade unionist, Socialist, Presidential Candidate, Jailed Anti-War Activist: Eugene Victor Debs was all of these and more. His career spanned two centuries from the Gilded Age into the roaring 1920s. Debs' radical presence was uniquely American.[4] More than half a century after this voice of the voiceless fell silent, the former railroad worker still has much to offer.[5] His ideas still advance a vision surprisingly relevant to the new millennium.

Born in Terre Haute, Indiana in 1855, Debs worked at a railroad engine house as a young man. Within a few years, young Gene was elevated to the position of locomotive fireman. Outwardly, his life appeared to follow the mythological American dream of consistent upward mobility. Soon, however, he became a force in the Brotherhood of Locomotive Firemen, the trade union representing his craft. He saw how railroad workers were separated from each other by numerous craft divisions. The divisions weakened the workers in their struggle against growing power of the Robber Barons from emerging American corporations.

Increasingly, Debs felt that all railroad workers needed to be organized into a single union with the power to protect labor from wage cutting and speed-ups. In 1893, the militant American Railroad Union (ARU) was born. The following year, George Pullman cut his

---

workers' wages while refusing to lower the rents they paid in his company town outside Chicago. The ARU voted not to handle scab Pullman cars and the battle lines were drawn.

Pullman had the support of other railroad owners as well as President Grover Cleveland. The union was hit with a federal injunction holding them in violation of the Sherman Anti-Trust Act. Illinois Governor John Peter Altgeld refused to mobilize the National Guard against the strike, so federal troops and hired thugs suppressed the striking workers. Because of his leadership during the strike, Eugene V. Debs served six months in the Woodstock, Illinois jail. He entered his cell a militant trade unionist and emerged a dedicated socialist.

What had happened in those six months? Debs was drawn to the teachings of Karl Marx, mainly supplied by Milwaukee Socialist Victor Berger.[6] They seemed to explain why America was the way it was —and why it should be changed. The writings of Karl Kautsky, often called the "Pope" of the Socialist International, made a strong impression on Debs as did many non-Marxist radicals including France's Victor Hugo. His reading also included Utopian works like Edward Bellamy's then popular *Looking Backward*.

When he left jail, Debs was convinced that capitalism—that is, the private ownership of the basic means of production and distribution—had to be abolished. He saw this step as the beginning, not the end, of a revolutionary process which would create a new society of free human beings. Opposed to all forms of oppression, the Socialist leader felt a kinship with all those run over by the wheels of, what the business press called, progress. When later sentenced for his anti-war stance, Debs commented "While there is a lower class I am in it, while there is a criminal element I am of it, and while there is a soul in prison I am not free."

While Gene Debs was the Socialist Party candidate for president five times (1900, 1904, 1908, 1912, 1920), he was surprisingly uninterested in winning votes. Rather he saw election campaigns as a way to promote socialist ideas and raise class consciousness. Nonetheless, nearly a million Americans marked their ballot for Debs in 1912[7] and again in 1920 when he ran from his Atlanta prison cell. The high point of Socialist electoral success was in 1912 when 1200 party members won office in two dozen different states.[8]

As a long time critic of The American Federation of Labor (AFL)'s emphasis on craft unionism, Debs was a supporter of industrial union-

---

ism and the object of AFL boss Samuel Gompers' contempt. Even within his tightly run AFL, Gompers faced a considerable Socialist bloc which was "always advocating independent political action and industrial unionism [and] as late as 1912 received 27 per cent of the vote when Max Hayes ran for president against Gompers."[9] When Debs and the Socialists leased a election campaign train, christened the "red special," Gompers charged that the costs had been paid by anti-labor interests trying "to split the labor vote."[10] In his largely successful effort to limit socialist influence within union members, Gompers roared "Socialism holds nothing but unhappiness for the human race. It destroys personal initiative, wipes out national pride--the heartstone of a people's culture--and finally it plays into the hands of the autocrats."[11]

By contrast, Debs supported the Industrial Workers of the World (IWW)[12] when they were established in 1905 and hoped that they would serve as an economic arm of the Socialist movement. He was soon disheartened by the predominance of syndicalist sentiment which emphasized direct action and spurned electoral activity.

When war broke out in Europe in August, 1914, Eugene V. Debs became very troubled. He had always thought that war was the world's worst terror and was disappointed in the many European socialists who voted to support their governments' war efforts. He dedicated himself to preventing American involvement in Europe's war. When, despite massive public opposition, the United States entered the war, the Socialist Party, the IWW (defended by Debs despite his political differences) and all anti-war activists were subject to a repression whose brutality is little paralleled in American history.

Seeing the flower of the radical movement being beaten and imprisoned, Debs stood with his jailed comrades. In 1918, Debs began a speaking tour which was a conscious provocation to President Woodrow Wilson and his administration. After giving a speech in Canton, Ohio, Debs was arrested by federal agents. At his trial, he refused to make a conventional defense but instead sought to publicize the unconstitutionality of the Espionage Act which was being used to silence the anti-war movement. His reward was a ten year sentence which the Supreme Court in *Debs v. United States* upheld despite of the obvious negation of the First Amendment.

While imprisoned, he sought to help his fellow inmates whose plight seemed to touch him more than his own.[13] He continued to receive votes as the Socialist Party candidate for President in 1920. Pardoned in late 1921 by President Warren G. Harding, he left his cell to re-enter a world where the Socialist Party and the radical movement lay in ruins. Although prison had taken its toll on the aged Debs, he labored to rebuild the American left. Despite his best efforts, the damage done by massive repression and bitter political schisms[14] prevented the Socialist Party from regaining its former momentum. Yet until the day he died in October 1926, Debs retained his sense of optimism and knowing that there was a new day coming.

—William A. Pelz
1 May 2000

[1] One example is Alexander Trachenberg's introduction to: *Speeches of Eugene V. Debs*, New York: International Publishers, 1928.

[2] In his introduction to one Debs anthology Arthur M. Schlesinger, Jr. goes so far as to have Debs play John the Baptist to Democratic President Franklin D. Roosevelt's Christ, *Writings and Speeches of Eugene V. Debs*, New York: Hermitage Press, 1948, p. xiii.

[3] For example, the introduction to: *Eugene V. Debs Speaks*, New York: Pathfinder Press, 1970.

[4] To further explore the life of this remarkable man, see the classic biography: Ray Ginger, *The Bending Cross: A Biography of Eugene Victor Debs*, New York: Russell & Russell, 1949 and the more recent scholarly work: Nick Salvatore, *Eugene V. Debs: Citizen and Socialist*, Urbana and Chicago: University of Illinois Press, 1982 as well as the useful: Bernard J. Brommel, *Eugene V. Debs: Spokesman for Labor and Socialism*, Chicago: Charles H. Kerr, 1978.

[5] For an excellent source of material showing his more private thoughts, there is the very worthwhile volume: J. Robert Constantine (editor), *Letters of Eugene V. Debs*, 3 vols., Urbana and Chicago: University of Illinois Press, 1990.

[6] For more on this Milwaukee Socialist, see: Sally M. Miller, *Victor Berger and the promise of Constructive Socialism, 1910-1920*, Westport, CN.: Greenwood Press, 1973.

[7] Nor were Party supporters only to be found among urban workers or immigrants, see: Garin Burbank, *When Farmers Voted Red: The Gospel of Socialism in the Oklahoma Countryside, 1910-1924*, Westport, CN.: Greenwood Press, 1976.

[8] See: Ira Kipnis, *The American Socialist Movement, 1897-1912*, New York: Columbia University Press, 1852; David A. Shannon, *The Socialist Party of America: a History*, Chicago: Quadrangle Books, 1967; Mari Jo Buhle, *Women and American Socialism*, Urbana, IL: University of Illinois Press, 1981.

[9] Richard O. Boyer and Herbert M. Morais, *Labor's Untold Story*, Pittsburgh: United Electrical Workers, 1955: 183.

[10] Samuel Gompers, *Seventy Years of Life and Labor: An Autobiography*, Vol. II, New York: E.P. Dutton & Company, 1925: 269.

[11] Gompers, Vol. II: 431.

[12] Their official history is: Fred W. Thompson and Patrick Murfin, *The I.W.W.: Its First Seventy Years, 1905-1975*, Chicago: Industrial Workers of the World, 1976.

[13] As a result of his experiences, the Socialist leader wrote a bitter attack on prisons and the system which made them necessary: Eugene V. Debs, *Walls and Bars*, Chicago: Charles H. Kerr, 1973.

[14] For details, consult: James Weinstein, *The Decline of Socialism in America, 1912-1925*, New York: Monthly Review Press, 1967.

Introduction

by Howard Zinn

"This selection of Debs' words will help introduce a new generation to an authentic American hero whose vision is as powerful today as in years past. Times have changed but the fundamental injustices which so moved Debs continue to cry out. If we seek to honor Eugene V. Debs, we should not lament his passing but, rather like him, organize."

We are always in need of radicals who are also lovable, and so we would do well to remember Eugene Victor Debs. Ninety years ago, at the time *The Progressive* was born, Debs was nationally famous as leader of the Socialist Party, and the poet James Whitcomb Riley wrote of him: "As warm a heart as ever beat Betwixt here and the Judgment Seat." Debs was what every socialist or anarchist or radical should be: fierce in his convictions, kind and compassionate in his personal relations. Sam Moore, a fellow inmate of the Atlanta penitentiary, where Debs was imprisoned for opposing the First World War, remembered how he felt as Debs was about to be released on Christmas Day, 1921: "As miserable as I was, I would defy fate with all its cruelty as long as Debs held my hand, and I was the most miserably happiest man on Earth when I knew he was going home Christmas."

Debs had won the hearts of his fellow prisoners in Atlanta. He had fought for them in a hundred ways and refused any special privileges for himself. On the day of his release, the warden ignored prison regulations and opened every cellblock to allow more than 2,000 inmates to gather in front of the main jail building to say goodbye to Eugene Debs. As he started down the walkway from the prison, a roar went up and he turned, tears streaming down his face, and stretched out his arms to the other prisoners.

This was not his first prison experience. In 1894, not yet a socialist but an organizer for the American Railway Union, he had led a nationwide boycott of the railroads in support of the striking workers at the Pullman Palace Car Company. They tied up the railroad system, burned hundreds of railway cars, and were met with the full force of the capitalist state: Attorney General Richard Olney, a former railroad lawyer, got a court injunction to prohibit blocking trains. President Cleveland called out the army, which used bayonets and rifle fire on a crowd of 5,000 strike sympathizers in Chicago. Seven hundred were arrested. Thirteen were shot to death.

Debs was jailed for violating an injunction prohibiting him from doing or saying anything to carry on the strike. In court, he denied he was a socialist, but during his six months in prison he read socialist literature, and the events of the strike took on a deeper meaning. He wrote later: "I was to be baptized in socialism in the roar of conflict.... In the gleam of every bayonet and the flash of every rifle the class struggle was revealed."

From then on, Debs devoted his life to the cause of working people and the dream of a socialist society. He stood on the platform with Mother Jones and Big Bill Haywood in 1905 at the founding convention of the Industrial Workers of the World. He was a magnificent speaker, his long body leaning forward from the podium, his arm raised dramatically. Thousands came to hear him talk all over the country.

With the outbreak of war in Europe in 1914 and the build-up of war fever against Germany, some socialists succumbed to the talk of "preparedness," but Debs was adamantly opposed. When President Wilson and Congress brought the nation into the war in 1917, speech was no longer free. The Espionage Act made it a crime to say anything that would discourage enlistment in the armed forces. Soon, close to 1,000 people were in prison for protesting the war. The producer of a movie called The Spirit of '76, about the American revolution, was sentenced to ten years in prison for promoting anti-British feeling at a time when England and the United States were allies. The case was officially labeled The US. v. The Spirit of '76.

Debs made a speech in Canton, Ohio, in support of the men and women in jail for opposing the war. He told his listeners: "Wars throughout history have been waged for conquest and plunder.... And that is war, in a nutshell. The master class has always declared the wars; the subject class has always fought the battles." He was found guilty and sentenced to ten years in prison by a judge who denounced those "who would strike the sword from the hand of this nation while she is engaged in defending herself against a foreign and brutal power."

In court, Debs refused to call any witnesses, declaring: "I have been accused of obstructing the war. I admit it. I abhor war. I would oppose war if I stood alone." Before sentencing, Debs spoke to judge and jury, uttering perhaps his most famous words. I was in his hometown of Terre Haute, Indiana, recently, among 200 people gathered to honor his memory, and we began the evening by reciting those words-words that moved me deeply when I first read them and move me deeply still: "While there is a lower class, I am in it. While there is a criminal element, I am of it. While there is a soul in prison, I am not free."

The "liberal" Oliver Wendell Holmes, speaking for a unanimous Supreme Court, upheld the verdict, on the ground that Debs's speech was intended to obstruct military recruiting. When the war was over, the "liberal" Woodrow Wilson turned down his Attorney General's recommendation that Debs be released, even though he was sixty-five and in poor health. Debs was in prison for thirty-two months. Finally, in 1921, the Republican Warren Harding ordered him freed on Christmas Day.

Today, when capitalism, "the free market," and "private enterprise" are being hailed as triumphant in the world, it is a good time to remember Debs and to rekindle the idea of socialism.

To see the disintegration of the Soviet Union as a sign of the failure of socialism is to mistake the monstrous tyranny created by Stalin for the vision of an egalitarian and democratic society that has inspired enormous numbers of people all over the world. Indeed, the removal of the Soviet Union as the false surrogate for the idea of socialism creates a great opportunity. We can now reintroduce genuine socialism to a world feeling the sickness of capitalism, its nationalist hatreds, its perpetual warfare, riches for a small number of people in a small number of countries, and hunger, homelessness, insecurity for everyone else.

Here in the United States we should recall that enthusiasm for socialism—production for use instead of profit, economic and social equality, solidarity with our brothers and sisters all over the world—was at its height before the Soviet Union came into being.

In the era of Debs, the first seventeen years of the twentieth century-until war created an opportunity to crush the movement-millions of Americans declared their adherence to the principles of socialism. Those were years of bitter labor struggles, the great walkouts of women garment workers in New York, the victorious multiethnic strike of textile workers in Lawrence, Massachusetts, the unbelievable courage of coal miners in Colorado, defying the power and wealth of the Rockefellers. The I.W.W. was born—revolutionary, militant, demanding "one big union" for everyone, skilled and unskilled, black and white, men and women, native-born and foreign-born.

More than a million people read *Appeal to Reason* and other socialist newspapers. In proportion to population, it would be as if today more than three million Americans read a socialist press. The party had 100,000 members, and 1,200 office-holders in 340 municipalities. Socialism was especially strong in the Southwest, among tenant farmers, railroad workers, coal miners, lumberjacks. Oklahoma had 12,000 dues paying members in 1914 and more than 100 socialists in local offices. It was the home of the fiery Kate Richards O'Hare. Jailed for opposing the war, she once hurled a book through a skylight to bring fresh air into the foul-smelling jail block, bringing cheers from her fellow inmates.

The point of recalling all this is to remind us of the powerful appeal of the socialist idea to people alienated from the political system and aware of the growing stark disparities in income and wealth—as so many Americans are today.

The word itself—socialism—may still carry the distortions of recent experience in bad places usurping the name. But anyone who goes around the country, or reads carefully the public opinion surveys over the past decade, can see that huge numbers of Americans agree on what should be the fundamental elements of a decent society: guaranteed food, housing, medical care for everyone; bread and butter as better guarantees of "national security" than guns and bombs; democratic control of corporate power; equal rights for all races, genders, and sexual orientations; a recognition of the rights of immigrants as the unrecognized counterparts of our parents and grandparents; the rejection of war and violence as solutions for tyranny and injustice.

There are people fearful of the word, all along the political spectrum. What is important, I think, is not the word, but a determination to hold up before a troubled public those ideas that are both bold and inviting-the more bold, the more inviting. That's what remembering Debs and the socialist idea can do for us.

This selection of Debs' words will help introduce a new generation to an authentic American hero whose vision is as powerful today as in years past. Times have changed but the fundamental injustices which so moved Debs continue to cry out. If we seek to honor Eugene V. Debs, we should not lament his passing but, rather like him, organize.

Howard Zinn, author of *A People's History of the United States*, wrote an earlier version of this essay in *The Progressive* magazine, 63(1), January 1999. (Those sections are reprinted with author's permission.)

The martyred apostles of labor

The century now closing is luminous with great achievements. In every department of human endeavor marvelous progress has been made. By the magic of the machine which sprang from the inventive genius of man, wealth has been created in fabulous abundance. But, alas, this wealth, instead of blessing the race, has been the means of enslaving it. The few have come in possession of all, and the many have been reduced to the extremity of living by permission.

A few have had the courage to protest. To silence these so that the dead-level of slavery could be maintained has been the demand and command of capital-blown power. Press and pulpit responded with alacrity. All the forces of society were directed against these pioneers of industrial liberty, these brave defenders of oppressed humanity—and against them the crime of the century has been committed.

Albert R. Parsons, August Spies, George Engel, Adolph Fischer, Louis Lingg, Samuel Fielden, Michael Schwab and Oscar Neebe paid the cruel penalty in prison cell and on the gallows.

They were the first martyrs in the cause of industrial freedom, and one of the supreme duties of our civilization, if indeed we may boast of having been redeemed from savagery, is to rescue their names from calumny and do justice to their memory.

The crime with which these men were charged was never proven against them. The trial which resulted in their conviction was not only a disgrace to all judicial procedure but a foul, black, indelible and damning stigma upon the nation.

It was a trial organized and conducted to convict—a conspiracy to murder innocent men, and hence had not one redeeming feature.

It was a plot, satanic in all its conception, to wreak vengeance upon defenseless men, who, not being found guilty of the crime charged in the indictment, were found guilty of exercising the inalienable right of free speech in the interest of the toiling and groaning masses, and thus they became the first martyrs to a cause which, fertilized by their blood, has grown in strength and sweep and influence from the day they yielded up their lives and liberty in its defense.

As the years go by and the history of that infamous trial is read and considered by men of thought, who are capable of wrenching themselves from the grasp of prejudice and giving reason its rightful supremacy, the stronger the conviction becomes that the present generation of workingmen should erect an enduring memorial to the men who had the courage to denounce and oppose wage-slavery and seek for methods of emancipation.

The vision of the judicially murdered men was prescient. They saw the dark and hideous shadow of coming events. They spoke words of warning, not too soon, not too emphatic, not too trumpet-toned—for even in 1886, when the Haymarket meetings were held, the capitalistic grasp was upon the throats of workingmen and its fetters were upon their limbs.

There was even then idleness, poverty, squalor, the rattling of skeleton bones, the sunken eye, the pallor, the living death of famine, the crushing and the grinding of the relentless mills of the plutocracy, which more rapidly than the mills of the gods grind their victims to dust.

The men who went to their death upon the verdict of a jury, I have said were judicially murdered—not only because the jury was packed for the express purpose of finding them guilty, not only because the crime for which they suffered was never proven against them, not only because the judge before whom they were arraigned was unjust and bloodthirsty, but because they had declared in the exercise of free speech that men who subjected their fellowmen to conditions often worse than death were unfit to live.

In all lands and in all ages where the victims of injustice have bowed their bodies to the earth, bearing grievous burdens laid upon them by cruel taskmasters, and have lifted their eyes starward in the hope of finding some orb whose light inspired hope, then million times the anathema has been uttered and will be uttered until a day shall dawn upon the world when the emancipation of those who toil is achieved by the brave, self-sacrificing few who, like the Chicago martyrs, have the courage of crusaders and the spirit of iconoclasts and dare champion the cause of the oppressed and demand in the name of an avenging God and of an outraged Humanity that infernalism shall be eliminated from our civilization.

And as the struggle for justice proceeds and the battlefields are covered with the slain, as Mother Earth drinks their blood, the stones are given tongues with which to denounce man's inhumanity to man—

aye, to women and children, whose moanings from hovel and sweatshop, garret and cellar, arraign our civilization, our religion and our judiciary—whose wailings and lamentations, hushing to silence every sound the Creator designed to make the world a paradise of harmonies, transform it into an inferno where the demons of greed plot and scheme to consign their victims to lower depths of degradation and despair.

The men who were judicially murdered in Chicago in 1887, in the name of the great State of Illinois, were the *avant-couriers* of a better day. They were called anarchists, but at their trial it was not proven that they had committed any crime or violated any law. They had protested against unjust laws and their brutal administration. They stood between oppressor and oppressed, and they dared, in a free (?) country, to exercise the divine right of free speech; and the record of their trial, as if written with an "iron pen and lead in the rock forever," proclaims the truth of the declaration.

I would rescue their names from slander. The slanderers of the dead are the oppressors of the living. I would, if I could, restore them to their rightful positions as evangelists, the proclaimers of good news to their fellow men—crusaders, to rescue the sacred shrines of justice from the profanations of the capitalistic defilers who have made them more repulsive than Aegean stables. Aye, I would take them, if I could, from peaceful slumber in their martyr graves—I would place them joint to joint in their dislocated necks—I would make the halter the symbol of redemption—I would restore the flesh to their skeleton bones—their eyes should again flash defiance to the enemies of humanity, and their tongues, again, more eloquent than all the heroes of oratory, should speak the truth to a gainsaying world. Alas, this cannot be done—but something can be done. The stigma fixed upon their names by an outrageous trial can be forever obliterated and their fame be made to shine with resplendent glory on the pages of history.

Until the time shall come, as come it will, when the parks of Chicago shall be adorned with their statues, and with holy acclaim, men, women and children, pointing to these monuments as testimonials of gratitude, shall honor the men who dared to be true to humanity and paid the penalty of their heroism with their lives, the preliminary work of setting forth their virtues devolves upon those who are capable of gratitude to men who suffered death that they might live.

They were the men who, like Al-Hassen, the minstrel of the king, went forth to find themes of mirth and joy with which to gladden the ears of his master, but returned disappointed, and, instead of themes to awaken the gladness and joyous echoes, found scenes which dried all the fountains of joy. Touching the golden harp, Al-Hassen sang to the king as Parsons, Spies, Engel, Fielden, Fischer, Lingg, Schwab and Neebe proclaimed to the people:

"O king, at thy Command I went into the world of men; I sought full earnestly the thing which I might weave into the gay and lightsome song. I found it, king; 'twas there. Had I the art to look but on the fair outside, I nothing else had found. That art not mine, I saw what lay beneath. And seeing thus I could not sing; for there, in dens more vile than wolf or jackal ever sought, were herded, stifling, foul, the writhing, crawling masses of mankind. Man! Ground down beneath Oppression's iron heel, till God in him was crushed and driven back, and only that which with the brute he shares finds room to upward grow."

Such pictures of horror our martyrs saw in Chicago, as others have seen them in all the great centers of population in the country. But, like the noble minstrel, they proceeded to recite their discoveries and with him moaned:

"And in this World I saw how womanhood's fair flower had never space its petals to unfold. How childhood's tender bud was crushed and trampled down in mire and filth too evil, foul, for beasts to be partakers in. For gold I saw the virgin sold, and Motherhood was made a mock and scorn.

"I saw the fruit of labor torn away from him who toiled, to further swell the bursting coffers of the rich, while babes and mothers pined and dies of want. I saw dishonor and injustice thrive. I saw the wicked, ignorant, greedy, and unclean, by means of bribes and baseness, raised to seats of power, from whence with lashes pitiless. And keen, they scourged the hungry, naked throng whom first they robbed and then enslaved."

Such were the scenes that the Chicago martyrs had witnessed and which may still be seen, and for reciting them and protesting against them they were judicially murdered.

It was not strange that the hearts of the martyrs "grew into one with the great moaning, throbbing heart" of the oppressed; not strange that the nerves of the martyrs grew "tense and quivering with the throes of mortal pain"; not strange that they should pity and plead and protest. The strange part of it is that in our high-noon of civilization a damnable judicial conspiracy should have been concocted to murder them under the forms of law.

That such is the truth of history, no honest man will attempt to deny; hence the demand, growing more pronounced every day, to snatch the names of these martyred evangelists of labor emancipation from dishonor and add them to the roll of the most illustrious dead of the nation.

—*The New Time*, February, 1898.

Prison labor

Its Effect on Industry and Trade

In my early years I stood before the open door of a blazing furnace and piled in the fuel to create steam to speed a locomotive along the iron track of progress and civilization. In the costume of the craft, through the grime of mingled sweat and smoke and dust, I was initiated into the great brotherhood of labor. The locomotive was my *alma mater*. I mastered the curriculum and graduated with the degree of D.D., not, as the lexicons interpret the letters, "Doctor of Divinity," but that better signification, "Do and Dare"—a higher degree than Aristotle conferred in his Lyceum or Plato thundered from his academy.

I am not in the habit of telling how little I know about Latin to those who have slaked their thirst for learning at the Pierian springs, but there is a proverb that has come down to us from the dim past which reads "Omnia vincit labor" and which has been adopted as the shibboleth of the American labor movement because, when reduced to English, it reads "Labor overcomes all things." In a certain sense this is true. Labor has built this great metropolis of the new world, built it as coral insects build the foundations of islands—build and die; build from the fathomless depth of the ocean until the mountain billows are dashed into spray as they beat against the fortifications beneath which the builders are forever entombed and forgotten.

Here in this proud city where wealth has built its monuments grander and more imposing than any of the seven wonders of the world named in classic lore, if you will excavate for facts you will find the remains, the bones of the toilers, buried and imbedded in their foundations. They lived, they wrought, they died. In their time they may have laughed and sung and danced to the music of their clanking chains. They married, propagated their species, and perpetuated conditions which, growing steadily worse, are today the foulest blots the imagination can conceive upon our much vaunted civilization.

And from these conditions there flow a thousand streams of vice and crime which have broadened and deepened until they constitute a perpetual menace to the peace and security of society. Jails, work-

---

houses, reformatories and penitentiaries have been crowded with victims, and the question how to control these institutions and their unfortunate inmates is challenging the most serious thought of the most advanced nations on the globe.

The particular phase of this grave and melancholy question which we are to consider this evening is embodied in the subject assigned the speakers: "Prison Labor, Its Effects on Industry and Trade."

I must confess that it would have suited my purpose better had the subject been transposed so as to read: "Industry and Trade, Their Effect on Labor," for, as a Socialist, I am convinced that the prison problem is rooted in the present system of industry and trade, carried forward, as it is, purely for private profit without the slightest regard to the effect upon those engaged in it, especially the men, women and children who perform the useful, productive labor which has created all wealth and all civilization.

Serious as is the problem presented in the subject of our discussion, it is yet insignificant when compared with the vastly greater question of the effect of our social and economic system upon industry and trade.

The pernicious effect of prison contract labor upon "free labor," so called, when brought into competition with it in the open market, is universally conceded, but it should not be overlooked that prison labor is itself an effect and not a cause, and that convict labor is recruited almost wholly from the propertyless, wage-working class that the inhuman system which has reduced a comparative few from enforced idleness to crime, has sunk the whole mass of labor to the dead level of industrial servitude.

It is therefore with the economic system, which is responsible for, not only prison labor, but for the gradual enslavement and degradation of all labor, that we must deal before there can be any solution of the prison labor problem or any permanent relief from its demoralizing influences.

But we will briefly consider the effect of prison labor upon industry and then pass to the larger question of the cause of prison labor and its appalling increase, to which the discussion logically leads.

From the earliest ages there has been a prison problem. The ancients had their bastilles and their dungeons. Most of the pioneers of progress, the haters of oppression, the lovers of liberty, whose names now glorify the pantheon of the world, made such institutions a necessity in their day. But civilization advances, however slowly, and there has been some progress. It required five hundred years to travel from the inquisition to the injunction.

In the earlier days punishment was the sole purpose of imprisonment. Offenders against the ruling class must pay the penalty in prison cell, which, not infrequently, was equipped with instruments of torture. With the civilizing process came the idea of the reformation of the culprit, and this idea prompts every investigation made of the latter-day problem. The inmates must be set to work for their own good, no less than for the good of the state.

It was at this point that the convict labor problem began and it has steadily expanded form that time to this and while there have been some temporary modifications of the evil, it is still an unmitigated curse from which there can be no escape while an economic system endures in which labor, that is to say the laborer, man, woman and child, is sold to the lowest bidder in the markets of the world.

More than thirty years ago Prof. E. C. Wines and Prof. Theodore W. Dwight, then commissioners of the Prison Association of New York, made a report to the legislature of the state on prison industry in which they said:

"Upon the whole it is our settled conviction that the contract system of convict labor, added to the system of political appointments, which necessarily involves a low grade of official qualification and constant changes in the prison staff, renders nugatory, to a great extent, the whole theory of our penitentiary system. Inspection may correct isolated abuses; philanthropy may relieve isolated cases of distress; and religion may effect isolated moral cures; but genuine, radical, comprehensive, systematic improvement is impossible."

The lapse of thirty years has not affected the wisdom or logic of the conclusion. It is as true now as it was then. Considered in his most favorable light, the convict is a scourge to himself, a menace to society and a burden to industry, and whatever system of convict labor may be tried, it will ultimately fail of its purpose at reformation of the criminal or the relief of industry as long as thousands of "free laborers," who have committed no crime, are unable to get work and make an honest living. Not long ago I visited a penitentiary in which a convict expressed regret that his sentence was soon to expire. Where was he to go, and what was he to do? And how long before he would

---

be sentenced to a longer term for a greater crime? The commission which investigated the matter in Ohio in 1877 reported to the legislature as follows:

"The contract system interferes in an undue manner with the honest industry of the state. It has been the cause of crippling the business of many of our manufacturers; it has been the cause of driving many of them out of business; it has been the cause of a large percentage of reductions which have taken place in the wages of our mechanics; it has been the cause of pauperizing a large portion of our laborers and increasing crime in a corresponding degree; it has been no benefit to the state; as a reformatory measure it has been a complete, total and miserable failure; it has hardened more criminals than any other cause; it has made total wrecks morally of thousands and thousands who would have been reclaimed from the paths of vice and crime under a proper system of prison management, but who have resigned their fate to a life of hopeless degradation; it has not a single commendable feature. Its tendency is pernicious in the extreme. In short, it is an insurmountable barrier in the way of the reformation of the unfortunates who are compelled to live and labor under its evil influences; it enables a class of men to get rich out of the crimes committed by others; it leaves upon the fair escutcheon of the state a relic of the very worst form of human slavery; it is a bone of ceaseless contention between the state and its mechanical and industrial interests; it is abhorred by all and respected by none except those, perhaps, who make profit and gain out of it. It should be tolerated no longer but abolished at once."

And yet this same system is still in effect in many of the states of the Union. The most revolting outrages have been perpetrated upon prison laborers under this diabolical system. Read the official reports and stand aghast at the atrocities committed against these morally deformed and perverted human creatures, your brothers and my brothers, for the private profit of capitalistic exploiters and the advancement of Christian civilization.

What a commentary on the capitalist competitive system! First, men are forced into idleness. Gradually they are driven to the extremity of begging or stealing. Having still a spark of pride and self-respect they steal and are sent to jail. The first sentence seals their doom. The brand of Cain is upon them. They are identified with the criminal class. Society, whose victims they are, has exiled them forever, and with this curse ringing in their ears they proceed on their downward career, sounding every note in the scale of depravity until at last, having graduated in crime all the way from petit larceny to homicide, their last despairing sign is wrung from them by the hangman's halter. From first to last these unfortunates, the victims of social malformation, are made the subjects of speculation and traffic. The barbed iron of the prison contractor is plunged into their quivering hearts that their torture may be coined into private profit for their exploiters.

In the investigation in South Carolina, where the convicts had been leased to railroad companies, the most shocking disclosures were made. Out of 285 prisoners employed by one company, 128, or more than 40 percent, died as the result, largely, of brutal treatment.

It is popular to say that society must be protected against its criminals. I prefer to believe that criminals should be protected against society, at least while we live under a system that makes the commission of crime necessary to secure employment.

The Tennessee tragedy is still fresh in the public memory. Here, as elsewhere, the convicts, themselves brutally treated, were used as a means of dragging the whole mine-working class down to their crime-cursed condition. The Tennessee Coal and Iron Company leased the convicts for the express purpose of forcing the wages of miners down to the point of subsistence. Says the official report: "The miners were compelled to work in competition with low-priced convict labor, the presence of which was used by the company as a scourge to force free laborers to its terms." Then the miners, locked out, their families suffering, driven to desperation, appealed to force and in a twinkling the laws of the state were trampled down, the authorities overpowered and defied, and almost five hundred convicts set at liberty.

Fortunately the system of leasing and contracting prison labor for private exploitation is being exposed and its rightful iniquities laid bare. Thanks to organized labor and to the spirit of prison reform, this horrifying phase of the evil is doomed to disappear before an enlightened public sentiment.

The public account system, though subject to serious criticism, is far less objectionable than either the lease, the contract or the price system. At least the prisoner's infirmities cease to be the prey of speculative greed and conscienceless rapacity.

The system of manufacturing for the use of state, country and municipal institutions, adopted by the state of New York, is an improvement upon those hitherto in effect, but it is certain to develop serious objections in course of time. With the use of modern machinery the limited demand will soon be supplied and then what? It may be in order to suggest that the prisoners could be employed in making shoes and clothes for the destitute poor and school books for their children and many other articles which the poor sorely need but are unable to buy.

Developing along this line it would be only a question of time until the state would be manufacturing all things for the use of the people, and then perhaps the inquiry would be pertinent: If the state can give men steady employment after they commit crime, and manufacturing can be carried forward successfully by their labor, why can it not give them employment before they are driven to that extremity, thereby preventing them from becoming criminals?

All useful labor is honest labor, even if performed in a prison. Only the labor of exploiters, such as speculators, stock gamblers, beef-embalmers and their mercenary politicians, lawyers and other parasites—only such is dishonest labor. A thief making shoes in a penitentiary is engaged in more useful and therefore more honest labor than a "free" stonemason at work on a palace whose foundations are laid in the skulls and bones, and cemented in the sweat and blood of ten thousand victims of capitalistic exploitation. In both cases the labor is compulsory. The stonemason would not work for the trustmagnate were he not compelled to.

In ancient times only slaves labored. And as a matter of fact only slaves labor now. The millions are made by the magic of manipulation. The coal miners of West Virginia, Pennsylvania, Ohio, Indiana and Illinois receive an average wage of less than seventy-five cents a day. They perform the most useful and necessary labor, without which your homes, if possible at all, would be cheerless as caves and the great heart of industry would cease to throb. Are they free men, or are they slaves? And what is the effect of *their* labor on trade and industry and upon themselves and their families? Dante would search the realms of inferno in vain for such pictures of horror and despair as are to be found in the mining regions of free America.

To the student of social science the haggard fact stands forth that under the competitive system of production and distribution the prison problem will never be solved—and its effect upon trade and industry will never be greatly modified. The fact will remain that whatever labor is performed by prison labor could and should be performed by free labor, and when in the march of economic progress the capitalist system of industry for private profit succumbs to the socialist system of industry for human happiness, when the factory, which is now a penitentiary crowded with life convicts, among whom children often constitute the majority—when this factory is transformed into a temple of science, and the machine, myriad-armed and tireless, is the only slave, there will be no prison labor and the problem will cease to vex the world, and to this it is coming in obedience to the economic law, as unerring in its operation as the law of gravitation.

That prison labor is demoralizing in its effect on trade and industry whenever and wherever brought into competition with it, especially under the various forms of the contract system, is of course conceded, but that it has been, or is at present, a great factor in such demoralization is not admitted. There is a tendency to exaggerate the blighting effects of prison labor for the purpose of obscuring the one overshadowing cause of demoralized trade and impoverished industry.

Prison labor did not reduce the miner to a walking hunger-pang, his wife to a tear-stained rag, and his home to a lair. Prison labor is not responsible for the squares of squalor and miles of misery in New York, Chicago and all other centers of population. Prison labor is not chargeable with the sweating dens in which the victims of capitalistic competition crouch in dread and fear until death comes to their rescue. Prison labor had no hand in Coeur d'Alene, Tennessee, Homestead, Hazleton, Virdin, Pana, that suburb of hell called Pullman and other ensanguined industrial battle fields where thousands of workingmen after being oppressed and robbed were imprisoned like felons, and shot down like vagabond dogs; where venal judges issued infamous injunctions and despotic orders at the behest of their masters, enforcing them with deputy marshals armed with pistols and clubs and supported by troops with gleaming bayonets and shotted

---

guns to drain the veins of workingmen of blood, but for whose labor this continent would still be a wilderness. Only the tortures of hunger and nakedness provoked protest, and this was silenced by the bayonet and bullet; by the club and the blood that followed the blow.

Prison labor is not accountable for the appalling increase in insanity, in suicide, in murder, in prostitution and a thousand other forms of vice and crime which pollute every fountain and contaminate every stream designed to bless the world.

Prison labor did not create our army of unemployed, but has been recruited from its ranks, and both owe their existence to the same social and economic system.

Nor are the evil effects confined exclusively to the poor working class. There is an aspect of the case in which the rich are as unfortunate as the poor. The destiny of the capitalist class is irrevocably linked with the working class. Fichte, the great German philosopher said, "Wickedness increases in proportion to the elevation of rank."

Prison labor is but one of the manifestations of our economic development and indicates its trend. The same cause that demoralized industry has crowded our prisons. Industry has not been impoverished by prison labor, but prison labor is the result of impoverished industry. The limited time at my command will not permit an analysis of the process.

The real question which confronts us is our industrial system and its effect upon labor. One of these effects is, as I have intimated, prison labor. What is its cause? What makes it necessary? The answer is: the competitive system, which creates wage-slavery, throws thousands out of employment and reduces the wages of thousands more to the point of bare subsistence.

Why is prison labor preferred to "free labor"? Simply because it is cheaper; it yields more profit to the man who buys, exploits and sells it. But this has its limitations. Capitalist competition that throngs the streets with idle workers, capitalist production that reduces human labor to a commodity and ultimately to crime—this system produces another kind of prison labor in the form of child labor which is being utilized more and more to complete the subjugation of the working class. There is this difference: The prison laborers are clothed and housed and fed. The child laborers whose wage is a dollar a week, or even less, must take care of themselves.

Prison labor is preferred because it is cheap. So with child labor.

It is not a question of prison labor, or of child labor, but of *cheap* labor.

Tenement-house labor is another form of prison labor.

The effects of cheap labor on trade and industry must be the same, whether such labor is done by prisoners, tenement house slaves, children or starving "hoboes."

The prison laborer produces by machinery in abundance but does not consume. The child likewise produces, but owing to its small wages, does not consume. So with the vast army of workers whose wage grows smaller as the productive capacity of labor increases, and then society is afflicted with overproduction, the result of underconsumption. What follows? The panic. Factories close down, wage-workers are idle and suffer, middle-class businessmen are forced into bankruptcy, the army of tramps is increased, vice and crime are rampant and prisons and work-houses are filled to overflowing as are sewers when the streets of cities are deluged with floods.

Prison labor, like all cheap labor, is at first a source of profit to the capitalist, but finally it turns into a two-edged sword that cuts into and destroys the system that produced it.

First, the capitalist pocket is filled by the employment of cheap labor—and then the bottom drops out of it.

In the cheapening process, the pauperized mass have lost their consuming power.

The case may now be summed up as follows:

First. Prison labor is bad; it has a demoralizing effect on capitalist trade and industry.

Second. Child labor, tenement house and every other form of cheap labor is bad; it is destructive of trade and industry.

Third. Capitalist competition is bad; it creates a demand for cheap labor.

Fourth. Capitalist production is bad; it creates millionaires and mendicants, economic masters and slaves, thus intensifying the class struggle.

This indicates that the present capitalist system has outlived its usefulness, and that it is in the throes of dissolution. Capitalism is but a link in the chain of social and economic development. Just as feudalism developed capitalism and then disappeared, so capitalism is now developing Socialism, and when the new social system has been completely evolved the last vestige of capitalism will fade into history.

The gigantic trust marks the change in production. It is no longer competitive but co-operative. The same mode of distribution, which must inevitably follow, will complete the process.

Co-operative labor will be the basis of the new social system, and this will be for use and not for profit. Labor will no longer be bought and sold. Industrial slavery will cease. For every man there will be the equal right to work with every other man and each will receive the fruit of his labor. Then we shall have economic equality. Involuntary idleness will be a horror of the past. Poverty will relax its grasp. The army of tramps will be disbanded because the prolific womb which now warms these unfortunates into life will become barren. Prisons will be depopulated and the prison labor problem will be solved.

Each labor-saving machine will lighten the burden and decrease the hours of toil. The soul will no longer be subordinated to the stomach. Man will live a complete life, and the march will then begin to an ideal civilization.

There is a proverb which the Latin race sent ringing down the centuries which reads, "Omnia vincit amor," or "Love conquers all things." Love and labor in alliance, working together, have transforming, redeeming and emancipating power. Under their benign sway the world can be made better and brighter.

Isaiah saw in prophetic vision a time when nations would war no more—when swords would be transformed into plowshares and spears into pruning hooks. The fulfillment of the prophecy only awaits an era when Love and Labor, in holy alliance, shall solve the economic problem.

Here, on this occasion, in this great metropolis with its thousand spires pointing heavenward, where opulence riots in luxury which challenges hyperbole, and poverty rots in sweat shops which only a Shakespeare or a Victor Hugo could describe, and the transfer to canvas would palsy the hand of a Michelangelo—here, where wealth and want and woe bear irrefutable testimony of deplorable conditions, I stand as a Socialist, protesting against the wrongs perpetrated upon Les Misèrables, and pleading as best I can for a higher civilization.

The army of begging Lazaruses, with the dogs licking their sores at the gates of palaces, where the rich are clothed in purple and fine linen with their tables groaning beneath the luxuries of all climes, make the palaces on the highland where fashion holds sway and music lends its charms, a picture in the landscape which, in illustrating disparity, brings into bolder relief the hut and the hovel in the hollow where want, gaunt and haggard, sits at the door and where light and plenty, cheerfulness and hope are forever exiled by the despotic decree of conditions as cruel as when the Czar of Russia orders to his penal mines in Siberia the hapless subjects who dare whisper the sacred word liberty—as cruel as when this boasted land of freedom commands that a far-away, innocent people shall be shot down in jungle and lagoon, in their bamboo huts, because they dream of freedom and independence.

These conditions are as fruitful of danger to the opulent as they are of degradation to the poor. It is neither folly nor fanaticism to assert that the country cannot exist under such conditions. The higher law of righteousness, of love and labor will prevail. It is a law which commends itself to reasoning men, a primal law enacted long before Jehovah wrote the dialogue amidst the thunders and lightnings of Sinai. It is a law written upon the tablets of every man's heart and conscience. It is a law infinitely above the creeds and dogmas and tangled disquisitions of the churches—the one law which in its operations will level humanity upward until men, redeemed from greed and every debasing ambition, shall obey its mandates and glory in its triumph.

Love and labor will give us the Socialist Republic—the Industrial Democracy—the equal rights of all men and women, and the emancipation of all from the vicious and debasing thraldoms of past centuries.

—Address before the Nineteenth Century Club at Delmonico's, New York City, March 21, 1899.

How I became a socialist

As I have some doubt about the readers of *The Comrade* having any curiosity as to "how I became a Socialist" it may be in order to say that the subject is the editor's, not my own; and that what is here offered is at his bidding—my only concern being that he shall not have cause to wish that I remained what I was instead of becoming a Socialist.

On the evening of February 27, 1875, the local lodge of the Brotherhood of Locomotive Firemen was organized at Terre Haute, Ind., by Joshua A. Leach, then grand master, and I was admitted as a charter member and at once chosen secretary. "Old Josh Leach," as he was affectionately called, a typical locomotive fireman of his day, was the founder of the brotherhood, and I was instantly attracted by his rugged honesty, simple manner and homely speech. How well I remember feeling his large, rough hand on my shoulder, the kindly eye of an elder brother searching my own as he gently said, "My boy, you're a little young, but I believe you're in earnest and will make your mark in the brotherhood." Of course, I assured him that I would do my best. What he really thought at the time flattered my boyish vanity not a little when I heard of it. He was attending a meeting at St. Louis some months later, and in the course of his remarks said: "I put a tow-headed boy in the brotherhood at Terre Haute not long ago, and some day he will be at the head of it."

Twenty-seven years, to a day, have played their pranks with "Old Josh" and the rest of us. When last we met, not long ago, and I pressed his good, right hand, I observed that he was crowned with the frost that never melts; and as I think of him now:

> "Remembrance wakes, with all her busy train,
> Swells at my breast and turns the past to pain."

My first step was thus taken in organized labor and a new influence fired my ambition and changed the whole current of my career. I was filled with enthusiasm and my blood fairly leaped in my veins. Day and night I worked for the brotherhood. To see its watchfires glow and observe the increase of its sturdy members were the sunshine and shower of my life. To attend the "meeting" was my supreme joy, and for ten years I was not once absent when the faithful assembled.

At the convention held in Buffalo in 1878 I was chosen associate editor of the magazine, and in 1880 I became grand secretary and treasurer. With all the fire of youth I entered upon the crusade which seemed to fairly glitter with possibilities. For eighteen hours at a stretch I was glued to my desk reeling off the answers to my many correspondents. Day and night were one. Sleep was time wasted and often, when all oblivious of her presence in the still small hours my mother's hand turned off the light. I went to bed under protest. Oh, what days! And what quenchless zeal and consuming vanity! All the firemen everywhere—and they were all the world—were straining:

> "To catch the beat
> On my tramping feet."

My grip was always packed; and I was darting in all directions. To tramp through a railroad yard in the rain, snow or sleet half the night, or till daybreak, to be ordered out of the roundhouse for being an "agitator," or put off a train, sometimes passenger, more often freight, while attempting to deadhead over the division, were all in the program, and served to whet the appetite to conquer. One night in midwinter at Elmira, N.Y., a conductor on the Erie kindly dropped me off in a snowbank, and as I clambered to the top I ran into the arms of a policemen, who heard my story and on the spot became my friend.

I rode on the engines over mountain and plain, slept in the cabooses and bunks, and was fed from their pails by the swarthy stokers who still nestle close to my heart, and will until it is cold and still.

Through all these years I was nourished at Fountain Proletaire. I drank deeply of its waters and every particle of my tissue became saturated with the spirit of the working class. I had fired an engine and been stung by the exposure and hardship of the rail. I was with the boys in their weary watches, at the broken engine's side and often helped to bear their bruised and bleeding bodies back to wife and child again. How could I but feel the burden of their wrongs? How could the seed of agitation fail to take deep root in my heart?

And so I was spurred on in the work of organizing, not the firemen merely, but the brakemen, switchmen, telegraphers, shopmen, track-hands, all of them in fact, and as I had now become known as

---

an organizer, the calls came from all sides and there are but few trades I have not helped to organize and less still in whose strikes I have not at some time had a hand.

In 1894 the American Railway Union was organized and a braver body of men never fought the battle of the working class.

Up to this time I had heard but little of Socialism, knew practically nothing about the movement, and what little I did know was not calculated to impress me in its favor. I was bent on thorough and complete organization of the railroad men and ultimately the whole working class, and all my time and energy were given to that end. My supreme conviction was that if they were only organized in every branch of the service and all acted together in concert they could redress their wrongs and regulate the conditions of their employment. The stockholders of the corporation acted as one, why not the men? It was such a plain proposition—simply to follow the example set before their eyes by their masters—surely they could not fail to see it, act as one, and solve the problem.

It is useless to say that I had yet to learn the workings of the capitalist system, the resources of its masters and the weakness of its slaves. Indeed, no shadow of a "system" fell athwart my pathway; no thought of ending wage-misery marred my plans. I was too deeply absorbed in perfecting wage-servitude and making it a "thing of beauty and a joy forever."

It all seems very strange to me now, taking a backward look, that my vision was so focalized on a single objective point that I utterly failed to see what now appears as clear as the noonday sun—so clear that I marvel that any workingman, however dull, uncomprehending, can resist it.

But perhaps it was better so. I was to be baptized in Socialism in the roar of conflict and I thank the gods for reserving to this fitful occasion the fiat, "Let there be light!"—the light that streams in steady radiance upon the roadway to the Socialist republic.

The skirmish lines of the A.R.U. were well advanced. A series of small battles was fought and won without the loss of a man. A number of concessions were made by the corporations rather than risk and encounter. Then came the fight on the Great Northern, short, sharp, and decisive. The victory was complete—the only railroad strike of magnitude ever won by an organization in America.

Next followed the final shock—the Pullman strike—and the American Railway Union again won, clear and complete. The combined corporations were paralyzed and helpless. At this juncture there was delivered, from wholly unexpected quarters, a swift succession of blows that blinded me for an instant and then opened wide my eyes— and in the gleam of every bayonet and the flash of every rifle *the class struggle was revealed*. This was my first practical lesson in Socialism, though wholly unaware that it was called by that name.

An army of detectives, thugs and murderers was equipped with badge and beer and bludgeon and turned loose; old hulks of cars were fired; the alarm bells tolled; the people were terrified; the most startling rumors were set afloat; the press volleyed and thundered, and over all the wires sped the news that Chicago's white throat was in the clutch of a red mob; injunctions flew thick and fast, arrests followed, and our office and headquarters, the heart of the strike, was sacked, torn out and nailed up by the "lawful" authorities of the federal government; and when in company with my loyal comrades I found myself in Cook County jail at Chicago with the whole press screaming conspiracy, treason and murder, and by some fateful coincidence I was given the cell occupied just previous to his execution by the assassin of Mayor Carter Harrison, Sr., overlooking the spot, a few feet distant, where the anarchists were hanged a few years before. I had another exceedingly practical and impressive lesson in Socialism.

Acting upon the advice of friends we sought to employ John Harlan, son of the Supreme Justice, to assist in our defense—a defense memorable to me chiefly because of the skill and fidelity of our lawyers, among whom were the brilliant Clarence Darrow and the venerable Judge Lyman Trumbull, author of the thirteenth amendment to the constitution, abolishing slavery in the United States.

Mr. Harlan wanted to think of the matter over night; and the next morning gravely informed us that he could not afford to be identified with the case, "for," said he, "you will be tried upon the same theory as were the anarchists, with probably the same result." That day, I remember, the jailer, by way of consolation, I suppose showed us the blood-stained rope used at the last execution and explained in minutest detail, as he exhibited the gruesome relic, just how the monstrous crime of lawful murder is committed.

But the tempest gradually subsided and with it the blood-thirstiness of the press and "public sentiment." We were not sentenced to the gallows, nor even to the penitentiary—though put on trial for conspiracy—for reasons that will make another story.

The Chicago jail sentences were followed by six months at Woodstock and it was here that Socialism gradually laid hold of me in its own irresistible fashion. Books and pamphlets and letters from Socialists came by every mail and I began to read and think and dissect the anatomy of the system in which workingmen, however organized, could be shattered and battered and splintered at a single stroke. The writings of Bellamy and Blatchford early appealed to me. The "Co-operative Commonwealth" of Gronlund also impressed me, but the writings of Kautsky were so clear and conclusive that I readily grasped, not merely his argument, but also caught the spirit of his Socialist utterance—and I thank him and all who helped me out of darkness into light.

It was at this time, when the first glimmerings of Socialism were beginning to penetrate, that Victor L. Berger—and I have loved him ever since—came to Woodstock, as if a providential instrument, and delivered the first impassioned message of Socialism I had ever heard—the very first to set the "wires humming in my system." As a souvenir of that visit there is in my library a volume of "Capital," by Karl Marx, inscribed with the compliments of Victor L. Berger, which I cherish as a token of priceless value.

The American Railway Union was defeated but not conquered—overwhelmed but not destroyed. It lives and pulsates in the Socialist movement, and its defeat but blazed the way to economic freedom and hastened the dawn of human brotherhood.

—*New York Comrade*, April, 1902.

What's the matter with Chicago?

For some days William E. Curtis, the far-famed correspondent of the Chicago *Record-Herald,* has been pressing the above inquiry upon representative people of all classes with a view to throwing all possible light upon that vexed subject.

The inquiry is in such general terms and takes such wide scope that anything like a comprehensive answer would fill a book without exhausting the subject, while a review of the "interviews" would embrace the whole gamut of absurdity and folly and produce a library of comedy and tragedy.

Not one of the replies I have seen has sufficient merit to be printed in a paper read by grown folks, and those that purport to come from leaders of labor and representatives of the working class take the prize in what would appear to be a competitive contest for progressive assininity.

The leader, so-called, who puts it upon record in a capitalist paper and gives the libel the widest circulation, that Chicago is alright, so far as the workers are concerned, that they have plenty and are prosperous and happy, is as fit to lead the working class as is a wolf to guide a flock of spring lambs.

It is from the wage worker's point of view that I shall attempt an answer to the question propounded by Mr. Curtis, and in dealing with the subject I shall be as candid as may be expected from a Socialist agitator.

The question is opportune at this season, when the "frost is on the pumpkin," and the ballot is soon to decide to what extent the people really know "What is the matter with Chicago."

First of all, Chicago is the product of modern capitalism, and, like all other great commercial centers, is unfit for human habitation. The Illinois Central Railroad Company selected the site upon which the city is built and this consisted of a vast miasmatic swamp far better suited to mosquito culture than for human beings. From the day the site was chosen by (and of course in the interest of all) said railway company, everything that entered into the building of the town and the development of the city was determined purely from profit considerations and without the remotest concern for the health and comfort of the human beings who were to live there, especially those who had to do all the labor and produce all the wealth.

As a rule hogs are only raised where they have good health and grow fat. Any old place will do to raise human beings.

At this very hour typhoid fever and diphtheria are epidemic in Chicago and the doctors agree that these ravages are due to the microbes and germs generated in the catchbasins and sewers which fester and exhale their foul and fetid breath upon the vast swarms of human beings caught and fettered there.

Thousands upon thousands of Chicago's population have been poisoned to death by the impure water and foul atmosphere of this undrainable swamp (notwithstanding the doctored mortuary tables by which it is proven to prospective investors that it is the healthiest city on earth) and thousands more will commit suicide in the same way, but to compensate for it all Chicago has the prize location for money-making, immense advantage for profit-mongering—and what are human beings compared to money?

During recent years Chicago has expended millions to lift herself out of her native swamp, but the sewage floats back to report the dismal failure of the attempt, and every germ-laden breeze confirms the report.

That is one thing that is the matter with Chicago. It never was intended that human beings should live there. A thousand sites infinitely preferable for a city could have been found in close proximity, but they lacked the "commercial" advantages which are of such commanding importance in the capitalist system.

And now they wonder "What is the Matter with Chicago!" Look at some of her filthy streets in the heart of the city, chronically torn up, the sunlight obscured, the air polluted, the water contaminated, every fountain and stream designed to bless the race poisoned at its source—and you need not wonder what ails Chicago, nor will you escape the conclusion that the case is chronic and that the present city will never recover from the fatal malady.

What is true of Chicago physically is emphasized in her social, moral and spiritual aspects, and this applies to every commercial metropolis in the civilized world.

From any rational point of view they are all dismal failures.

There is no reason under the sun, aside form the profit considerations of the capitalist system, why two million humans should be stacked up in layers and heaps until they jar the clouds, while millions of acres of virgin soil are totally uninhabited.

The very contemplation of the spectacle gives rise to serious doubt as to the sanity of the race.

Such a vast population in such a limited area cannot feed itself, has not room to move and cannot keep clean.

The deadly virus of capitalism is surging through all the veins of this young mistress of trade and the eruptions are found all over the body social and politic, and that's "What's the matter with Chicago."

Hundreds of the *Record-Herald's* quacks are prescribing their nostrums for the blotches and pustules which have broken out upon the surface, but few have sense enough to know and candor enough to admit that the virus must be expelled from the system—and these few are Socialists who are so notoriously visionary and impracticable that their opinions are not worthy of space in a great paper printed to conserve the truth and promote the welfare of society.

This model metropolis of the West has broken all the records for political corruption. Her old rival on the Mississippi, catching the inspiration doubtless, has been making some effort to crown herself with similar laurels, but for smooth political jobbery and fancy manipulation of the wires, Chicago is still far in the lead. In the "Windy City" ward politics has long been recognized as a fine art and the collection is unrivaled anywhere.

From the millions of dollars filched from the millions of humans by the corporate owners of the common utilities, the reeking corruption funds flow like lava tides, and to attempt to purify the turbid stream by the "reform measures" proposed from time to time by the Republican-Democratic Party in its internal conflict for the spoils of office, is as utter a piece of folly as to try with beeswax to seal up Mount Pelèe.

Chicago has plutocrats and paupers in the ratio of more than sixteen to one—boulevards for the exhibition of the rich and alleys for the convenience of the poor.

Chicago has also a grand army of the most skilled pickpockets, artistic confidence operators, accomplished foot-pads and adept cracksmen on earth. So well is this understood that on every breeze we hear the refrain:

"When Reuben comes to town,
He's sure to be done brown—"

And this lugubrious truth is treated as the richest of jokes, with utter unconsciousness of the moral degeneracy it reflects, the crime it glorifies and the indictment of capitalist society it returns in answer to the *Record-Herald's* query: "What's the matter with Chicago"?

Besides the array of "talent" above mentioned, fostered by competitive society everywhere, the marshy metropolis by the lake may boast of a vast and flourishing gambling industry, an illimitable and progressive "levee" district, sweatshops, slums, dives, bloated men, bedraggled women, ghastly caricatures of their former selves, babies cradled in rags and filth, aged children, than which nothing could be more melancholy—all those and a thousand more, the fruit of our present social anarchy, afflict Chicago; and worst of all, our wise social philosophers, schooled in the economics of capitalist universities, preach the comforting doctrine that all these are necessary evils and at best can but be restricted within certain bounds; and this hideous libel is made a cloak that theft may continue to masquerade as philanthropy.

It is at this point that Chicago particularly prides herself upon her "charities," hospitals and eleemosynary endowments, all breathing the sweet spirit of Christian philanthropy—utterly ignorant of the fact, designedly or otherwise, that these very institutions are manifestations of social disease and are monumental of the iniquity of the system that must rear such whited sepulchres to conceal its crimes.

I do not oppose the insane asylum—but I abhor and condemn the cut-throat system that robs man of his reason, drives him to insanity and makes the lunatic asylum an indispensable adjunct to every civilized community.

With the ten thousand "charities" that are proposed to poultice the sores and bruises of society, I have little patience.

Worst of all is the charity ball. Chicago indulges in these festering festivals on a grand scale.

Think of cavorting around in a dress suit because some poor wretch is hungry; and of indulging in a royal carousal to comfort some despairing woman on the brink of suicide; and finally, that in "fashionable society" the definition of this mixture of inanity and moral perversion is "charity."

Fleece your fellows! That is "business," and you are a captain of industry. Having "relieved" your victims of their pelts, dance and make merry to "relieve" their agony. This is "charity" and you are a philanthropist.

In summing up the moral assets of a great (?) city, the churches should not be overlooked. Chicago is a city of fine churches. All the denominations are copiously represented, and sermons in all languages and of all varieties are turned out in job lots and at retail to suit the market.

The churches are always numerous where vice is rampant. They seem to spring from the same soil and thrive in the same climate.

And yet the churches are supposed to wage relentless warfare upon evil. To just what extent they have checked its spread in the "Windy City" may be inferred from the probing of the press into the body social to ascertain "What is the matter with Chicago."

The preachers are not wholly to blame, after all, for their moral and spiritual impotency. They are wage-workers, the same as coal miners, and are just as dependent upon the capitalist class. How can they be expected to antagonize the interests of their employers and hold their jobs? The unskilled preachers, the common laborers in the arid spots of the vineyard, are often wretchedly paid, and yet they remain unorganized and have never struck for better wages.

"What's the matter with Chicago"? Capitalism!

What's the cure? Socialism!

Regeneration will only come with depopulation—when Socialism has relieved the congestion and released the people and they spread out over the country and live close to the grass.

The *Record-Herald* has furnished the people of Chicago and Illinois with a campaign issue.

If you want to know more about "What is the matter with Chicago," read the Socialist papers and magazines; read the platform of the Socialist Party; and if you do, you will cut loose from the Republican-Democratic Party, the double-headed political monstrosity of the capitalist class and you will cast your vote for the Socialist Party and your lot with the International Socialist Movement, whose mission it is to uproot and overthrow the whole system of capitalist exploitation, and put an end to the poverty and misery it entails—and that's "What's the matter with Chicago."

—*Chicago Socialist,* October 25, 1902.

The negro in class struggle

I t so happens that I write upon the Negro question, in compliance with the request of the editor of the *International Socialist Review*, in the state of Louisiana, where the race prejudice is as strong and the feeling against the "nigger" as bitter and relentless as when Lincoln's proclamation of emancipation lashed the waning Confederacy into fury and incited the final and desperate attempts to burst the bonds that held the southern states in the federal union. Indeed, so thoroughly is the south permeated with the malign spirit of race hatred that even Socialists are to be found, and by no means rarely, who either share directly in the race hostility against the Negro, or avoid the issue, or apologize for the social obliteration of the color line in the class struggle.

The white man in the south declares that "the nigger is all right in his place"; that is, as menial, servant and slave. If he dare hold up his head, feel the thrill of manhood in his veins and nurse the hope that some day may bring deliverance; if in his brain the thought of freedom dawns and in his heart the aspiration to rise above the animal plane and propensities of his sires, he must be made to realize that notwithstanding the white man is civilized (?) the black man is a "nigger" still and must so remain as long as planets wheel in space.

But while the white man is considerate enough to tolerate the Negro "in his place," the remotest suggestion at social recognition arouses all the pent-up wrath of his Anglo-Saxon civilization; and my observation is that the less real ground there is for such indignant assertion of self-superiority, the more passionately it is proclaimed.

At Yoakum, Texas, a few days ago, leaving the depot with two grips in my hands, I passed four or five bearers of the white man's burden perched on a railing and decorating their environment with tobacco juice. One of them, addressing me, said: "There's a nigger that'll carry your grips." A second one added: "That's what he's here for," and the third chimed in with "That's right, by God." Here was a savory bouquet of white superiority. One glance was sufficient to satisfy me that they represented all there is of justification for the implacable hatred of the Negro race. They were ignorant, lazy, unclean, totally void of ambition, themselves the foul product of the capitalist system and held in lowest contempt by the master class, yet esteeming themselves immeasurable above the cleanest, most intelligent and self-respecting Negro, having by reflex absorbed the "nigger" hatred of their masters.

As a matter of fact the industrial supremacy of the south before the war would not have been possible without the Negro, and the south of today would totally collapse without his labor. Cotton culture has been and is the great staple and it will not be denied that the fineness and superiority of the fibre that makes the export of the southern states the greatest in the world is due in large measure to the genius of the Negroes charged with its cultivation.

The whole word is under obligation to the Negro, and that the white heel is still upon the black neck is simply proof that the world is not yet civilized.

The history of the Negro in the United States is a history of crime without a parallel.

Why should the white man hate him? Because he stole him from his native land and for two centuries and a half robbed him of the fruit of his labor, kept him in beastly ignorance and subjected him to the brutal domination of the lash? Because, he tore the black child from the breast of its mother and ravished the black man's daughter before her father's eyes?

There are thousands of Negroes who bear testimony in their whitening skins that men who so furiously resent the suggestion of "social equality" are far less sensitive in respect to the sexual equality of the races.

But of all the senseless agitation in capitalist society, that in respect to "social equality" takes the palm. The very instant it is mentioned the old aristocratic plantation owner's shrill cry about the "buck nigger" marrying the "fair young daughter" of his master is heard from the tomb and echoed and re-echoed across the spaces and repeated by the "white trash" in proud vindication of their social superiority.

Social equality, forsooth! Is the black man pressing his claims for social recognition upon his white burden bearer? Is there any reason why he should? Is the white man's social recognition of his own white brother such as to excite the Negro's ambition to cover the noble prize? Has the Negro any greater desire, or is there any reason why he should have, for social intercourse with the white man than the white man has for social relations with the Negro? This phase of the Negro question is pure fraud and serves to mask the real issue, which is not *social equality*, BUT ECONOMIC FREEDOM.

There never was any social inferiority that was not the shriveled fruit of economic inequality.

The Negro, given economic freedom, will not ask the white man any social favors; and the burning question of "social equality" will disappear like mist before the sunrise.

I have said and say again that, properly speaking, there is no Negro question outside of the labor question—the working class struggle. Our position as Socialists and as a party is perfectly plain. We have simply to say: "The class struggle is colorless." The capitalists, white black and other shades, are on one side and the workers, white, black and all other colors, on the other side.

When Marx said: "Workingmen of all countries unite," he gave concrete expression to the socialist philosophy of the class struggle; unlike the framers of the Declaration of Independence who announced that "all men are created equal" and then basely repudiated their own doctrine, Marx issued the call to all the workers of the globe, regardless of race, sex, creed or any other condition whatsoever.

As a social party we receive the Negro and all other races upon absolutely equal terms. We are the party of the working class, the whole working class, and we will not suffer ourselves to be divided by any specious appeal to race prejudice; and if we should be coaxed or driven from the straight road we will be lost in the wilderness and ought to perish there, for we shall no longer be a Socialist Party.

Let the capitalist press and capitalist "public opinion" indulge themselves in alternate flattery and abuse of the Negro; we as Socialists will receive him in our party, treat him in our counsels and stand by him all around the same as if his skin were white instead of black; and this we do, not from any considerations of sentiment, but because it accords with the philosophy of Socialism, the genius of the class struggle, and is eternally right and bound to triumph in the end.

With the "nigger" question, the "race war" from the capitalist viewpoint we have nothing to do. In capitalism the Negro question is a grave one and will grow more threatening as the contradictions and complications of capitalist society multiply, but this need not worry us. Let them settle the Negro question in their way, if they can. We have nothing to do with it, for that is their fight. We have simply to open the eyes of as many Negroes as we can and bring them into the Socialist movement to do battle for emancipation from wage slavery, and when the working class have triumphed in the class struggle and stand forth economic as well as political free men, the race problem will forever disappear.

Socialists should with pride proclaim their sympathy with and fealty to the black race, and if any there be who hesitate to avow themselves in the face of ignorant and unreasoning prejudice, they lack the true spirit of the slavery-destroying revolutionary movement.

The voice of Socialism must be as inspiring music to the ears of those in bondage, especially the weak black brethren, doubly enslaved, who are bowed to the earth and groan in despair beneath the burden of the centuries.

For myself, my heart goes to the Negro and I make no apology to any white man for it. In fact, when I see the poor, brutalized, outraged black victim, I feel a burning sense of guilt for his intellectual poverty and moral debasement that makes me blush for the unspeakable crimes committed by my own race.

In closing, permit me to express the hope that the next convention may repeal the resolutions on the Negro question. The Negro does not need them and they serve to increase rather than diminish the necessity for explanation.

We have nothing special to offer the Negro, and we cannot make separate appeals to all the races.

The Socialist Party is the party of the working class, regardless of color—the whole working class of the whole world.

—*International Socialist Review*, November, 1903.

The negro and his nemesis

Since the appearance of my article on "The Negro in the Class Struggle" in the November *Review* I have received the following anonymous letter:

Elgin, Ill., November 25, 1903.
Mr. Debs:

Sir, I am a constant reader of the *International Socialist Review*. I have analyzed your last article on the Negro question with apprehension and fear. You say that the South is permeated with the race prejudice of the Negro more than the North. I say it is not so. When it comes right down to a test, the North is more fierce in the race prejudice of the Negro than the South ever has been or ever will be. I tell you, you will jeopardize the best interests of the Socialist Party if you insist on political equality of the Negro. For that will not only mean political equality but also social equality eventually. I do not believe you realize what that means. You get social and political equality for the Negro, then let him come and ask the hand of your daughter in marriage, "For that seems to be the height of his ambition," and we will see whether you still have a hankering for social and political equality for the Negro. For I tell you, the Negro will not be satisfied with equality with reservation. It is impossible for the Anglo-Saxon and the African to live on equal terms. You try it, and he will pull you down to his level. Mr. Lincoln, himself, said, that "There is a physical difference between the white and black races, which I believe will forever forbid them living together on terms of social and political equality." If the Socialist leaders *stoop* to this method to gain votes, then their policy and doctrine is as rotten and degraded as that of the Republican and Democratic parties, and I tell you, if the resolutions are adopted to give the African equality with the Anglo-Saxon you will lose more votes than you now think. I for my part shall do all I can to make you lose as many as possible and there will be others. For don't you know that just a little sour dough will spoil the whole batch of bread. You will do the Negro a greater favor by leaving him where he is. You elevate and educate him, and you will make his position impossible in the U.S.A. Mr. Debs, if you have any doubt on this subject, I beg you for humanity's sake to read Mr. Thomas Dixon's "The Leopard's Spots" and I hope that all others who have voiced your sentiments heretofore, will do the same.

I assure you, I shall watch the *International Socialist Review* with the most intense hope of a reply after you have read Mr. Thomas Dixon's message to humanity. Respectfully yours,
So far a staunch member of the Socialist Party.

The writer, who subscribes himself "A staunch member of the Socialist Party" is the only member of that kind I have ever heard of who fears to sign his name to, and accept responsibility for what he writes. The really "staunch" Socialist attacks in the open—he does not shoot from ambush.

The anonymous writer, as a rule, ought to be ignored, since he is unwilling to face those he accuses, while he may be a sneak or coward, traitor or spy, in the role of a "staunch Socialist," whose base design it is to divide and disrupt the movement. For reasons which will appear later, this communication is made an exception and will be treated as if from a known party member in good standing.

It would be interesting to know of what branch our critic is a member and how long he has been, and how he happened to become a "staunch member of the Socialist Party." That he is entirely ignorant of the philosophy of Socialism may not be to his discredit, but that a "staunch member" has not even read the platform of his party not only admits of no excuse, but takes the "staunchness" all out of him, punctures and discredits his foolish and fanatical criticism and leaves him naked and exposed to ridicule and contempt.

The Elgin writer has all the eminent and well recognized qualifications necessary to oppose Negro equality. His criticism and the spirit that prompts it harmonize delightfully with his assumed superiority.

That he may understand that he claims to be a "staunch member" of a party he knows nothing about I here incorporate the "Negro Resolutions" adopted by our last national convention, which constitute a vital part of the national platform of the Socialist Party and clearly defined its attitude toward the Negro:

NEGRO RESOLUTION

Whereas, The Negroes of the United States, because of their long training in slavery and but recent emancipation therefrom, occupy a peculiar position in the working class and in society at large;

Whereas, The capitalist class seeks to preserve this peculiar condition, and to foster and increase color prejudice and race hatred between the white worker and the black, so as to make their social and economic interests to appear to be separate and antagonistic, in order that the workers of both races may thereby be more easily and completely exploited;

Whereas, Both the old political parties and educational and religious institutions alike betray the Negro in his present helpless struggle against disfranchisement and violence, in order to receive the economic favors of the capitalist class. Be it, therefore,

Resolved, That we, the Socialists of America, in national convention assembled, do hereby assure our Negro fellow worker of our sympathy with him in his subjection to lawlessness and oppression, and also assure him of the fellowship of the workers who suffer from the lawlessness and exploitation of capital in every nation or tribe of the world. Be it further

Resolved, That we declare to the Negro worker the identity of his interests and struggles with the interests and struggle of the workers of all lands, without regard to race or color or sectional lines; that the causes which have made him the victim of social and political inequality are the effects of the long exploitation of his labor power; that all social and race prejudices spring from the ancient economic causes which still endure, to the misery of the whole human family, that the only line of division which exists in fact is that between the producers and the owners of the world—between capitalism and labor. And be it further

Resolved, That we the American Socialist Party, invite the Negro to membership and fellowship with us in the world movement for economic emancipation by which equal liberty and opportunity shall be secured to every man and fraternity become the order of the world.

But even without this specific declaration, the position of the party is so clear that no member and no other person of ordinary intelligence can fail to comprehend it.

The Socialist Party is the congealed, tangible expression of the Socialist movement, and the Socialist movement is based upon the modern class struggle in which all workers of all countries, regardless of race, nationality, creed or sex, are called upon to unite against the capitalist class, their common exploiter and oppressor. In this great class struggle the economic equality of all workers is a foregone conclusion, and he who does not recognize and subscribe to it as one of the basic principles of the Socialist philosophy is not a Socialist, and if a party member must have been admitted through misunderstanding or false pretense, he should be speedily set adrift, that he may return to the capitalist parties with their social and economic strata from the "white trash" and "buck nigger" *down* to the syphilitic snob and harlot heiress who barters virtue for title in the matrimonial market.

I did not say that the race prejudice in the South was more intense than in the North. No such comparison was made and my critic's denial is therefore unnecessary upon this point. Whether the prejudice of the South differs from that of the North is quite another question and entirely aside from the one at issue, not is it of sufficient interest to consider at this time.

The Elgin writer says that we shall "jeopardize the best interests of the Socialist Party" if we insist upon the political equality of the Negro. I say that the Socialist Party would be false to its historic mission, violate the fundamental principles of Socialism, deny its philosophy and repudiate its own teachings if, on account of race considerations, it sought to exclude any human being from political equality and economic freedom. Then, indeed, would it not only "jeopardize" its best interests, but forfeit its very life, for it would soon be scorned and deserted as a thing unclean, leaving but a stench in the nostrils of honest men.

Political equality is to be denied the Negro, according to this writer, because it would lead to social equality, and this would be terrible—especially for those "white" men who are already married to Negro women and those "white" women who have long since picked the "buck nigger" in preference to the "white trash" whose social superiority they were unable to distinguish or appreciate.

The negro and his nemesis

Of course the Negro will "not be satisfied with equality with reservation." Why should he be? Would you?

Suppose you change places with the Negro just a year, then let us hear from you—"with reservation."

What now follows it is difficult to consider with patience: "You get social and political equality for the Negro, then let him come and ask the hand of your daughter in marriage."

In the first place *you* don't get equality for the Negro—*you* haven't got it yourself. In the present social scale there is no difference between you and the Negro—you are on the same level in the labor market, and the capitalist whose agent buys your labor power doesn't know and doesn't care if you are white or black, for he deals with you simply as *labor power*, and is uninterested save as to the quality and quantity you can supply. He cares no more about the color of your hide than does Armour about that of the steers he buys in the cattle market.

In the next place the Negro will fight for his own political and economic equality. He will take his place in the Socialist Party with the workers of all colors and all countries, and all of them will unite in the fight to destroy the capitalist system that now makes common slaves of them all.

Foolish and vain indeed is the workingman who makes the color of his skin the stepping-stone to his imaginary superiority. The trouble is with his head, and if he can get that right he will find that what ails him is not superiority but inferiority, and that he, as well as the Negro he despises, is the victim of wage-slavery, which robs him of what he produces and keeps both him and the Negro tied down to the dead level of ignorance and degradation.

As for "the Negro asking the hand of your daughter in marriage," that is so silly and senseless that the writer is probably after all justified in withholding his name. How about the daughter asking the hand of the Negro in marriage? Don't you know this is happening every day? Then, according to your logic, inferiority and degeneracy of the white race is established and the Negro ought to rise in solemn protest against political equality, lest the white man ask the hand of his daughter in marriage.

"It is impossible," continues our critic, "for the Anglo-Saxon and the African to live upon equal terms. You try it and he will pull you down to his level." Our critic must have tried something that had a downward pull, for surely that is his present tendency.

The fact is that it is impossible for the Ango-Saxon and the African to live on *unequal* terms. A hundred years of American history culminiating in the Civil War proves that. Does our correspondent want a repetition of the barbarous experiment?

How does the Anglo-Saxon get along with the Anglo-Saxon—leaving the Negro entirely out of the question? Do they bill and coo and love and caress each other? Is the Anglo-Saxon capitalist so devoted to his Anglo-Saxon wage-slave that he shares his burden and makes him the equal partner of his wealth and joy? Are they not as widely separated as the earth and sky, and do they not fight each other to the death? Does not the white capitalist look down with contempt upon the white wage-slave? And don't you know that the plutocrat would feel himself pretty nearly, if not quite as outrageously insulted to have his Anglo-Saxon wage slave ask the hand of his daughter in marriage as if that slave were black instead of white?

Why are you not afraid that some Anglo-Saxon engine-wiper on the New York Central will ask the hand of Vanderbilt's daughter in marriage?

What social distinction is there between a white and a black deckhand on a Mississippi steamboat? Is it visible even with the aid of a microscope? They are both slaves, work side by side, sometimes a bunch of black slaves under a white "boss" and at other times a herd of white slaves under a black "boss." Not infrequently you have to take a second look to tell them apart—but all are slaves and all are humans and all are robbed by their "superior" white brother who attends church, is an alleged follower of Jesus Christ and has a horror of "social equality." To him "a slave is a slave for a' that"—when he bargains for labor power he is not generally concerned about the color of the package, but if he is, it is to give the black preference because it can be bought at a lower price in the labor market, in which equality always prevails—the equality of intellectual and social debasement. To paraphrase Wordsworth:

"A wage-slave by the river's brim
A simple wage-slave is to him
And he is nothing more."

The negro and his nemesis

The man who seeks to arouse race prejudice among workingmen is not their friend. He who advises the white wage-worker to look down upon the black wage-worker is the enemy of both.

The capitalist has some excuse for despising the slave—he lives out of his labor, out of his life, and cannot escape his sense of guilt, and so he looks with contempt upon his victim.

You can forgive the man who robs you, but you can't forgive the man you rob—in his haggard features you read your indictment and this makes his face so repulsive that you must keep it under your heels where you cannot see it.

One need not experiment with "sour dough" nor waste any time on "sour" literature turned into "Leopard Spots" to arrive at sound conclusions upon these points, and the true Socialist delights not only in taking his position and speaking out, but in inviting and accepting without complaint all the consequences of his convictions, be they what they may.

Abraham Lincoln was a noble man, but he was not an abolitionist, and what he said in reference to the Negro was with due regard to his circumscribed environs, and, for the time, was doubtless the quintessence of wisdom, but he was not an oracle who spoke for all coming ages, and we are not bound by what he thought prudent to say in a totally different situation half a century ago.

The Socialist platform has not a word in reference to "social equality." It declares in favor of political and economic equality, and only he who denies this to any other human being is unfit for it.

Socialism will give all men economic freedom, equal opportunity to work, and the full product of their labor. Their "social" relations they will be free to regulate to suit themselves. Like religion this will be an individual matter and our Elgin Negro-hater can consider himself just as "superior" as he chooses, confine his social attentions exclusively to white folks, and enjoy his leisure time in hunting down the black spectre who is bent on asking his daughter's hand in marriage.

What warrant has he to say that the height of the Negro's ambition is to marry a white woman? No more than a Negro has to say that the height of a white woman's ambition is to marry a Negro. The number of such cases is about equally divided and it is so infinitesimally small that any one who can see danger to society in it ought to have his visual organs treated for progressive exaggeration.

The normal Negro has ambition to rise. This is to his credit and ought to be encouraged. He is not asking, nor does he need, the white man's social favors. He can regulate his personal associations with entire satisfaction to himself, without Anglo-Saxon concessions.

Suppose another race as much "superior" to the white as the white is to the black should drop from the skies. Would our Illinois correspondent at once fall upon his knees and acknowledge his everlasting inferiority, or would he seek to overcome it and rise to the higher plane of his superiors?

The Negro, like the white man, is subject to the laws of physical, mental and moral development. But in his case these laws have been suspended. Socialism simply proposes that the Negro shall have full opportunity to develop his mind and soul, and this will in time emancipate the race from animalism, so repulsive to those especially whose fortunes are built up out of it.

The African is here and to stay. How came he to our shores? Ask your grandfathers, Mr. Anonymous, and if they will tell the truth you will or should blush for their crimes.

The black man was stolen from his native land, from his wife and child, brought to these shores and made a slave. He was chained and whipped and robbed by his "white superior," while the son of his "superior" raped the black child before his eyes. For centuries he was kept in ignorance and debased and debauched by the white man's law.

The rape-fiend? Horrible!

Whence came he! Not by chance. He can be accounted for. Trace him to his source and you will find an Anglo-Saxon at the other end. There are no rape-maniacs in Africa. They are the spawn of civilized lust.

Anglo-Saxon civilization is reaping and will continue to reap what it has sown.

For myself, I want no advantage over my fellow man and if he is weaker than I, all the more is it my duty to help him.

Nor shall my door or my heart be ever closed against any human being on account of the color of his skin.

International Socialist Review, January, 1904.

The socialist party and the working class

Mr. Chairman, Citizens and Comrades:

There has never been a free people, a civilized nation, a real republic on this earth. Human society has always consisted of masters and slaves, and the slaves have always been and are today, the foundation stones of the social fabric.

Wage-labor is but a name; wage-slavery is the fact.

The twenty-five millions of wage-workers in the United States are twenty-five millions of twentieth-century slaves.

This is the plain meaning of what is known as

THE LABOR MARKET.

And the labor market follows the capitalist flag.

The most barbarous fact in all Christendom is the labor market. The mere term sufficiently expresses the animalism of commercial civilization.

They who buy and they who sell in the labor market are alike dehumanized by the inhuman traffic in the brains and blood and bones of human beings.

The labor market is the foundation of so-called civilized society. Without these shambles, without this commerce in human life, this sacrifice of manhood and womanhood, this barter of babes, this sale of souls, the capitalist civilizations of all lands and all climes would crumble to ruin and perish from the earth.

Twenty-five millions of wage-slaves are bought and sold daily at prevailing prices in the American Labor Market.

This is the

PARAMOUNT ISSUE

in the present national campaign.

Let me say at the very threshold of this discussion that the workers have but the one issue in this campaign, the overthrow of the capitalist system and the emancipation of the working class from wage-slavery.

The capitalists may have the tariff, finance, imperialism and other dust-covered and moth-eaten issues entirely to themselves.

The rattle of these relics no longer deceives workingmen whose heads are on their own shoulders.

They know by experience and observation that the gold standard, free silver, fiat money, protective tariff, free trade, imperialism and anti-imperialism all mean capitalist rule and wage-slavery.

Their eyes are open and they can see; their brains are in operation and they can think.

The very moment a workingman begins to do his own thinking he understands the paramount issue, parts company with the capitalist politician and falls in line with his own class on the political battlefield.

The political solidarity of the working class means the death of despotism, the birth of freedom, the sunrise of civilization.

Having said this much by way of introduction I will now enter upon the actualities of my theme.

THE CLASS STRUGGLE.

We are entering tonight upon a momentous campaign. The struggle for political supremacy is not between political parties merely, as appears upon the surface, but at bottom it is a life and death struggle between two hostile economic classes, the one the capitalist, and the other the working class.

The capitalist class is represented by the Republican, Democratic, Populist and Prohibition parties, all of which stand for private ownership of the means of production, and the triumph of any one of which will mean continued wage-slavery to the working class.

As the Populist and Prohibition sections of the capitalist party represent minority elements which propose to reform the capitalist system without disturbing wage-slavery, a vain and impossible task, they will be omitted from this discussion with all the credit due the rank and file for their good intentions.

The Republican and Democratic parties, or to be more exact, the Republican-Democratic Party, represent the capitalist class in the class struggle. They are the political wings of the capitalist system and such differences as arise between them relate to spoils and not to principles.

With either of these parties in power one thing is always certain and that is the capitalist class is in the saddle and the working class under the saddle.

Under the administration of both these parties the means of production are private property, production is carried forward for capitalist profit purely, markets are glutted and industry paralyzed, workingmen become tramps and criminals while injunctions, soldiers and riot guns are brought into action to preserve "law and order" in the chaotic carnival of capitalistic anarchy.

Deny it as may the cunning capitalists who are clear-sighted enough to perceive it, or ignore it as may the torpid workers who are too blind and unthinking to see it, the struggle in which we are engaged today is a class struggle, and as the toiling millions come to see and understand it and rally to the political standard of their class, they will drive all capitalist parties of whatever name into the same party and the class struggle will then be so clearly revealed that the hosts of labor will find their true place in the conflict and strike the united and decisive blow that will destroy slavery and achieve their full and final emancipation.

In this struggle the workingmen and women and children are represented by the Socialist Party and it is my privilege to address you in the name of that revolutionary and uncompromising party of the working class.

ATTITUDE OF THE WORKERS.

What shall be the attitude of the workers of the United States in the present campaign? What part shall they take in it? What party and what principles shall they support by their ballots? And why?

These are questions the importance of which are not sufficiently recognized by workingmen or they would not be the prey of parasites and the service tools of scheming politicians who use them only at election time to renew their masters' lease of power and perpetuate their own ignorance, poverty and shame.

In answering these questions I propose to be as frank and candid as plain-meaning words will allow, for I have but one object in this discussion and that object is not office, but the truth, and I shall state it as I see it, if I have to stand alone.

But I shall not stand alone, for the party that has my allegiance and may have my life, the Socialist Party, the party of the working class, the party of emancipation, is made up of men and women who know their rights and scorn to compromise with their oppressors; who want no votes that can be bought and no support under any false pretense whatsoever.

The Socialist Party stands squarely upon its proletarian principles and relies wholly upon the forces of industrial progress and the education of the working class.

The Socialist Party buys no votes and promises no office. Not a farthing is spent for whiskey or cigars. Every penny in the campaign fund is the voluntary offerings of workers and their sympathizers and every penny is used for education.

What other parties can say the same?

Ignorance alone stands in the way of Socialist success. The capitalist parties understand this and use their resources to prevent the workers from seeing the light.

Intellectual darkness is essential to industrial slavery.

Capitalist parties stand for Slavery and Night.

The Socialist Party is uniting them upon the living issue;

Death to Wage Slavery!

When industrial slavery is as dead as the issues of the Siamese-twin capitalist parties the Socialist Party will have fulfilled its mission and enriched history.

And now to our questions:

First, all workingmen and women owe it to themselves, their class and their country to take an active and intelligent interest in political affairs.

THE BALLOT.

The ballot of united labor expresses the people's will and the people's will is the supreme law of a free nation.

The ballot means that labor is no longer dumb, that at last it has a voice, that it may be heard and if united shall be heeded.

Centuries of struggle and sacrifice were required to wrest this symbol of freedom from the mailed clutch of tyranny and place it in the hand of labor as the shield and lance of attack and defense.

The abuse and not the use of it is responsible for its evils.

The divided vote of labor is the abuse of the ballot and the penalty is slavery and death.

The united vote of those who toil and have not will vanquish those who have and toil not, and solve forever the problem of democracy.

THE HISTORIC STRUGGLE OF CLASSES.

Since the race was young there have been class struggles. In every state of society, ancient and modern, labor has been exploited, degraded and in subjection.

Civilization has done little for labor except to modify the forms of its exploitation.

Labor has always been the mudsill of the social fabric—is so now and will be until the class struggle ends in class extinction and free society.

Society has always been and is now built upon exploitation—the exploitation of a class—the working class, whether slaves, serfs or wage-laborers, and the exploited working class in subjection have always been, instinctively or consciously, in revolt against their oppressors.

Through all the centuries the enslaved toilers have moved slowly but surely toward their final freedom.

The call of the Socialist Party is to the exploited class, the workers in all useful trades and professions, all honest occupations, from the most menial service to the highest skill, to rally beneath their own standard and put an end to the last of the barbarous class struggles by conquering the capitalist government, taking possession of the means of production and making them the common property of all, abolishing wage-slavery and establishing the co-operative commonwealth.

The first step in this direction is to sever all relations with

CAPITALIST PARTIES.

They are precisely alike and I challenge their most discriminating partisans to tell them apart in relation to labor.

The Republican and Democratic parties are alike capitalist parties—differing only in being committed to different sets of capitalist interests—they have the same principles under varying colors, are equally corrupt and are one in their subservience to capital and their hostility to labor.

The ignorant workingman who supports either of these parties forges his own fetters and is the unconscious author of his own misery. He can and must be made to see and think and act with his fellows in supporting the party of his class and this work of education is the crowning virtue of the Socialist movement.

THE REPUBLICAN PARTY.

Let us briefly consider the Republican Party from the worker's standpoint. It is capitalist to the core. It has not and can not have the slightest interest in labor except to exploit it.

Why should a workingman support the Republican Party?

Why should a millionaire support the Socialist Party?

For precisely the same reason that all the millionaires are opposed to the Socialist Party, all the workers should be opposed to the Republican Party. It is a capitalist party, is loyal to capitalist interests and entitled to the support of capitalist voters on election day.

All it has for workingmen is its "glorious past" and a "glad hand" when it wants their votes.

The Republican Party is now and has been for several years, in complete control of government.

What has it done for labor? What has it not done for capital?

Not one of the crying abuses of capital has been curbed under Republican rule.

Not one of the petitions of labor has been granted.

The eight hour and anti-injunction bills, upon which organized labor is a unit, were again ruthlessly slain by the last Congress in obedience to the capitalist masters.

David M. Parry has greater influence at Washington than all the millions of organized workers.

Read the national platform of the Republican Party and see if there is in all its bombast a crumb of comfort for labor. The convention that adopted it was a capitalist convention and the only thought it had of labor was how to abstract its vote without waking it up.

In the only reference it made to labor it had to speak easy so as to avoid offense to the capitalists who own it and furnish the boodle to keep it in power.

The labor platforms of the Republican and Democratic parties are interchangeable and non-redeemable. They both favor "justice to capital and justice to labor." This hoary old platitude is worse than meaningless. It is false and misleading and so intended. Justice to labor means that labor shall have what it produces. This leaves nothing for capital.

Justice to labor means the end of capital.

The old parties intend nothing of the kind. It is false pretense and false promise. It has served well in the past. Will it continue to catch the votes of unthinking and deluded workers?

What workingmen had part in the Republican national convention or were honored by it?

The grand coliseum swarmed with trust magnates, corporation barons, money lords, stock gamblers, professional politicians, lawyers, lobbyists and other plutocratic tools and mercenaries, but there

---

was no room for the horny-handed and horny-headed sons of toil. They built it but were not in it.

Compare that convention with the convention of the Socialist Party, composed almost wholly of working men and women and controlled wholly in the interest of their class.

But a party is still better known by its chosen representatives than by its platform declarations.

Who are the nominees of the Republican Party for the highest offices in the gift of the nation and what is their relation to the working class?

First of all, Theodore Roosevelt and Charles W. Fairbanks, candidates for President and Vice-President, respectively, deny the class struggle and this almost infallibly fixes their status as friends of capital and enemies of labor. They insist that they can serve both; but the fact is obvious that only one can be served and that one at the expense of the other. Mr. Roosevelt's whole political career proves it.

The capitalists made no mistake in nominating Mr. Roosevelt. They know him well and he has served them well. They know that his instincts, associations, tastes and desires are with them, that he is in fact one of them and that he has nothing in common with the working class.

The only evidence to the contrary is his membership in the Brotherhood of Locomotive Firemen which seems to have come to him co-incident with his ambition to succeed himself in the presidential chair. He is a full-fledged member of the union, has the grip, signs and passwords; but it is not reported that he is attending meetings, doing picket duty, supporting strikes and boycotts and performing such other duties as his union obligation imposes.

When Ex-President Grover Cleveland violated the Constitution and outraged justice by seizing the state of Illinois by the throat and handcuffing her civil administration at the behest of the crime-stained trusts and corporations, Theodore Roosevelt was among his most ardent admirers and enthusiastic supporters. He wrote in hearty commendation of the atrocious act, pronounced it most exalted patriotism and said he would have done the same himself had he been president.

And so he would and so he will!

How impressive to see the Rough Rider embrace the Smooth Statesman! Oyster Bay and Buzzard's Bay! "Two souls with but a single thought, two hearts that beat as one."

There is also the highest authority for the statement charging Mr. Roosevelt with declaring about the same time he was lauding Cleveland that if he was in command he would have such as Altgeld, Debs and other traitors lined up against a dead wall and shot. The brutal remark was not for publication but found its way into print and Mr. Roosevelt, after he became a candidate, attempted to make denial, but the words themselves sound like Roosevelt and bear the impress of his savage visage.

Following the Pullman strike in 1894, there was an indignant and emphatic popular protest against "government by injunction," which has not yet by any means subsided.

Organized labor was, and is, a unit against the insidious form of judicial usurpation as a means of abrogating constitutional restraints of despotic power.

Mr. Roosevelt with his usual zeal to serve the ruling class and keep their slaves in subjection, vaulted into the arena and launched his tirade upon the "mob" that dared oppose the divine rule of a corporate judge.

"Men who object to what they style 'government by injunction,' " said he, "are, as regards the essential principles of government, in hearty sympathy with their remote skin-clad ancestors, who lived in caves, fought one another with stone-headed axes and ate the mammoth and woolly rhinoceros. They are dangerous whenever there is the least danger of their making the principles of this ages-buried past living factors in our present life. They are not in sympathy with men of good minds and good civic morality."

In direct terms and plain words Mr. Roosevelt denounces all those who oppose "Government by Injunction" as cannibals, barbarians and anarchists, and this violent and sweeping stigma embraces the whole organized movement of labor, every man, woman and child that wears the badge of union labor in the United States.

It is not strange in the light of these facts that the national Congress, under President Roosevelt's administration, suppresses anti-injunction and eight-hour bills and all other measures favored by labor and resisted by capital.

No stronger or more convincing proof is required of Mr. Roosevelt's allegiance to capital and opposition to labor, nor of the class struggle and class rule which he so vehemently denies; and the workingman who in the face of these words and acts, can still sup-

---

port Mr. Roosevelt, must feel himself flattered in being publicly proclaimed a barbarian, and sheer gratitude, doubtless, impels him to crown his benefactor with the highest honors.

If the working class are barbarians, according to Mr. Roosevelt, this may account for his esteeming himself as having the very qualities necessary to make himself Chief of the Tribe.

But it must be noted that Mr. Roosevelt denounced organized labor as savages long before he was a candidate for president. After he became a candidate he joined the tribe and is today, himself, according to his own dictum, a barbarian and the enemy of civic morality.

The labor union to which President Roosevelt belongs and which he is solemnly obligated to support, is unanimously opposed to "Government by Injunction." President Roosevelt knew it when he joined it and he also knew that those who oppose injunction rule have the instincts of cannibals and are a menace to morality, but his proud nature succumbed to political ambition, and his ethical ideas vanished as he struck the trail that led to the tribe and, after a most dramatic scene and impressive ceremony, was decorated with the honorary badge of international barbarism.

How Theodore Roosevelt, the trade-unionist, can support the presidential candidate who denounced him as an immoral and dangerous barbarian, he may decided at his leisure, and so may all other union men in the United States who are branded with the same vulgar stigma, and their ballots will determine if they have the manhood to resent insult and rebuke its author, or if they have been fitly characterized and deserve humiliation and contempt.

The appointment of Judge Taft to a cabinet position is corroborative evidence, if any be required, of President Roosevelt's fervent faith in Government by Injunction. Judge Taft first came into national notoriety when, some years ago, sitting with Judge Ricks, who was later tried for malfeasance, they issued the celebrated injunction during the Toledo, Ann Arbor & North Michigan railroad strike that paralyzed the Brotherhoods of Locomotive Engineers and Firemen and won for them the gratitude and esteem of every corporation in the land. They were hauled to Toledo, the headquarters of the railroad, in a special car, pulled by a special engine, on special time, and after hastily consulting the railroad magnates and receiving instructions, let go the judicial lightning that shivered the unions to splinters and ended the strike in total defeat. Judge Taft is a special favorite with the trust barons and his elevation to the cabinet was ratified with joy at the court of St. Plutus.

Still again did President Roosevelt drive home his arch-enmity to labor and his implacable hostility to the trade-union movement when he made Paul Morton, the notorious union hater and union wrecker, his secretary of the navy. That appointment was an open insult to every trade-unionist in the country and they who lack the self-respect to resent it at the polls may wear the badge, but they are lacking wholly in the spirit and principles of union labor.

Go ask the brotherhood men who were driven from the C. B. & Q. and the striking union machinists on the Santa Fe to give you the pedigree of Mr. Morton and you will learn that his hate for union men is equaled only by his love for the scabs who take their places.

Such a man and such another as Sherman Bell, the military ferret of the Colorado mine owners, are the ideal patriots and personal chums of Mr. Roosevelt, and by honoring these he dishonors himself and should be repudiated by the ballot of every working man in the nation.

Mr. Fairbanks, the Republican candidate for Vice-President, is a corporation attorney of the first class and a plutocrat in good and regular standing. He is in every respect a fit and proper representative of his party and every millionaire in the land may safely support him.

THE DEMOCRATIC PARTY.

In referring to the Democratic Party in this discussion we may save time by simply saying that since it was born again at the St. Louis convention it is near enough like its Republican ally to pass for a twin brother.

The former party of the "common people" is no longer under the boycott of the plutocracy since it has adopted the Wall Street label and renounced its middle class heresies.

The radical and progressive element of the former Democracy have been evicted and must seek other quarters. They were an unmitigated nuisance in the conservative counsels of the old party. They were for the "common people" and the trusts have no use for such a party.

Where but to the Socialist Party can these progressive people turn? They are now without a party and the only genuine Democratic Party in the field is the Socialist Party, and every true Democrat should thank Wall Street for driving him out of a party that is democratic in name only and into one that is democratic in fact.

The St. Louis convention was a trust jubilee. The Wall Street reorganizers made short work of the free silver element. From first to last it was a capitalistic convocation. Labor was totally ignored. As an incident, two thousand choice chairs were reserved for the Business Men's League of St. Louis, an organization hostile to organized labor, but not a chair was tendered to those whose labor had built the convention hall, had clothed, transported, fed and wined the delegates and whose votes are counted on as if they were so many dumb driven cattle, to pull the ticket through in November.

As another incident, when Lieutenant Richmond Hobson dramatically declared that President Cleveland had been the only president who had ever been patriotic enough to use the federal troops to crush union labor, the trust agents, lobbyists, tools and clackers screamed with delight and the convention shook with applause.

The platform is precisely the same as the Republican platform in relation to labor. It says nothing and means the same. A plank was proposed condemning the outrages in Colorado under Republican administration, but upon order from the Parryites it was promptly thrown aside.

The editor of *American Industries* organ of the Manufacturers' Association, commented at length in its issue of July 15 on the triumph of capital and the defeat of labor at both Republican and Democratic national conventions. Among other things he said: "The two labor lobbies, partly similar in make-up, were, to put it bluntly, thrown out bodily in both places." And that is the simple fact and is known of all men who read the papers. The capitalist organs exult because labor, to use their own brutal expression, was kicked bodily out of both the Republican and Democratic national conventions.

What more than this is needed to open the eyes of workingmen to the fact that neither of these parties is their party and that they are as strangely out of place in them as Rockefeller and Vanderbilt would be in the Socialist Party?

And how many more times are they to be "kicked out bodily" before they stay out and join the party of their class in which labor is not only honored but is supreme, a party that is clean, that has conscience and convictions, a party that will one day sweep the old parties from the field like chaff and issue the Proclamation of Labor's Emancipation?

Judge Alton B. Parker corresponds precisely to the Democratic platform. It was made to order for him. His famous telegram in the expiring hour removed the last wrinkle and left it a perfect fit.

Thomas W. Lawson, the Boston millionaire, charges that Senator Patrick McCarren, who brought out Judge Parker for the nomination, is on the payroll of the Standard Oil company as political master mechanic at twenty thousand dollars a year, and that Parker is the chosen tool of Standard Oil. Mr. Lawson offers Senator McCarren one hundred thousand dollars if he will disprove the charge.

William Jennings Bryan denounced Judge Parker as a tool of Wall Street before he was nominated and declared that no self-respecting Democrat could vote for him, and after his nomination he charged that it had been dictated by the trusts and secured by "crooked and indefensible methods." Mr. Bryan also said that labor had been betrayed in the convention and need look for nothing from the Democratic Party. He made many other damaging charges against his party and its candidates, but when the supreme test came he was not equal to it, and instead of denouncing the betrayers of the "common people" and repudiating their made-to-order Wall Street program, he compromised with the pirates that scuttled his ship and promised with his lips the support his heart refused and his conscience condemned.

The Democratic nominee for President was one of the Supreme Judges of the State of New York who declared the eight-hour law unconstitutional and this is an index of his political character.

In his address accepting the nomination he makes but a single allusion to labor and in this he takes occasion to say that labor is charged with having recently used dynamite in destroying property and that the perpetrators should be subjected to "the most rigorous punishment known to the law." This cruel intimation amounts to conviction in advance of trial and indicates clearly the trend of his capitalistically trained judicial mind. He made no such reference to capital, nor to those ermined rascals who use judicial dynamite in blowing up the Constitution while labor is looted and starved by capitalistic freebooters who trample all law in the mire and leer and mock at their despoiled and helpless victims.

It is hardly necessary to make more than passing reference to Henry G. Davis, Democratic candidate for Vice-President. He is a coal baron, railroad owner and, of course, and enemy to union labor. He has amassed a great fortune exploiting his wage-slaves and has always strenuously resisted every attempt to organize them for the

---

betterment of their condition. Mr. Davis is a staunch believer in the virtue of the injunction as applied to union labor. As a young man he was in charge of a slave plantation and his conviction is that wage-slaves should be kept free from the contaminating influence of the labor agitator and render cheerful obedience to their master.

Mr. Davis is as well qualified to serve his party as is Senator Fairbanks to serve the Republican party and wage-workers should have no trouble in making their choice between this pernicious pair of plutocrats, and certainly no intelligent workingman will hesitate an instant to discard them both and cast his vote for Ben Hanford, their working class competitor, who is as loyally devoted to labor as Fairbanks and Davis are to capital.

THE SOCIALIST PARTY.

In what has been said of other parties I have tried to show why they should not be supported by the common people, least of all by workingmen, and I think I have shown clearly enough that such workers as do support them are guilty, consciously or unconsciously, of treason to their class. They are voting into power the enemies of labor and are morally responsible for the crimes thus perpetrated upon their fellow-workers and sooner or later they will have to suffer the consequences of their miserable acts.

The Socialist Party is not, and does not pretend to be, a capitalist party. It does not ask, nor does it expect the votes of the capitalist class. Such capitalists as do support it do so seeing the approaching doom of the capitalist system and with a full understanding that the Socialist Party is not a capitalist party, nor a middle class party, but a revolutionary working class party, whose historic mission it is to conquer capitalism on the political battle-field, take control of government and through the public powers take possession of the means of wealth production, abolish wage-slavery and emancipate all workers and all humanity.

The people are as capable of achieving their industrial freedom as they were to secure their political liberty, and both are necessary to a free nation.

The capitalist system is no longer adapted to the needs of modern society. It is outgrown and fetters the forces of progress. Industrial and commercial competition are largely of the past. The handwriting blazes on the wall. Centralization and the combination are the modern forces in industrial and commercial life. Competition is breaking down and co-operation is supplanting it.

The hand tools of early times are used no more. Mammoth machines have taken their places. A few thousand capitalists own them and many millions of workingmen use them.

All the wealth the vast army of labor produces above its subsistence is taken by the machine owning capitalists, who also own the land and the mills, the factories, railroads and mines, the forests and fields and all other means of production and transportation.

Hence wealth and poverty, millionaires and beggars, castles and caves, luxury and squalor, painted parasites on the boulevard and painted poverty among the red lights.

Hence strikes, boycotts, riots, murder, suicide, insanity, prostitution on a fearful and increasing scale.

The capitalist parties can do nothing. They are a part, an iniquitous part, of the foul and decaying system.

There is no remedy for the ravages of death.

Capitalism is dying and its extremities are already decomposing. The blotches upon the surface show that the blood no longer circulates. The time is near when the cadaver will have to be removed and the atmosphere purified.

In contrast with the Republican and Democratic conventions, where politicians were the puppets of plutocrats, the convention of the Socialist Party consisted of workingmen and women fresh from their labors, strong, clean, wholesome, self-reliant, ready to do and dare for the cause of labor, the cause of humanity.

Proud indeed am I to have been chosen by such a body of men and women to bear aloft the proletarian standard in this campaign and heartily do I endorse the clear and cogent platform of the party which appeals with increasing force and eloquence to the whole working class of the country.

To my associate upon the national ticket I give my hand with all my heart. Ben Hanford typifies the working class and fitly represents the historic mission and revolutionary character of the Socialist Party.

CLOSING WORDS.

These are stirring days for living men. The day of crisis is drawing near and Socialists are exerting all their power to prepare the people for it.

The old order of society can survive but little longer. Socialism is next in order. The swelling minority sounds warning of the impending change. Soon that minority will be the majority and then will come the co-operative commonwealth.

Every workingman should rally to the standard of his class and hasten the full-orbed day of freedom.

Every progressive Democrat must find his way in our direction and if he will but free himself from prejudice and study the principles of Socialism he will soon be a sturdy supporter of our party.

Every sympathizer with labor, every friend of justice, every lover of humanity should support the Socialist Party as the only party that is organized to abolish industrial slavery, the prolific source of the giant evils that afflict the people.

Who with a heart in his breast can look upon Colorado without keenly feeling the cruelties and crimes of capitalism! Repression will not help her. Brutality will only brutalize her. Private ownership and wage-slavery are the curse of Colorado. Only Socialism will save Colorado and the nation.

The overthrow of capitalism is the object of the Socialist Party. It will not fuse with any other party and it would rather die than compromise.

The Socialist Party comprehends the magnitude of its task and has the patience of preliminary defeat and the faith of ultimate victory.

The working class must be emancipated by the working class.

Woman must be given her true place in society by the working class.

Child labor must be abolished by the working class.

Society must be reconstructed by the working class.

The working class must be employed by the working class.

The fruits of labor must be enjoyed by the working class.

War, bloody war, must be ended by the working class.

These are the principles and objects of the Socialist Party and we fearlessly proclaim them to our fellowmen.

We know our cause is just and that it must prevail.

With faith and hope and courage we hold our heads erect and with dauntless spirit marshal the working class for the march from Capitalism to Socialism, from Slavery to Freedom, from Barbarism to Civilization.

—Opening speech delivered as candidate of the
Socialist Party for President, at Indianapolis, Ind.,
September 1, 1904.

An ideal labor press

The prime consideration in the present industrial system is profit. All other things are secondary. Profit is the life blood of capital—the vital current of the capitalist system, and when it shall cease to flow the system will be dead.

The capitalist is the owner of the worker's tools. Before the latter can work he must have access to the capitalist's tool-house and permission to use the master's tools. What he produces with these tools belongs to the master, to whom he must sell his labor power at the market price. The owner of the tools is therefore master of the man.

Only when the capitalist can exact a satisfactory profit from his labor power is the worker given a job, or allowed to work at all.

Profit first; labor, life, love, liberty—all these must take second place.

In such a system labor is in chains, and the standard of living, if such it may be called, is corner-stoned in crusts and rags.

Under such conditions ideas and ideals are not prolific among the sons and daughters of toil.

Slavery does not excite lofty aspirations nor inspire noble ideals. The tendency is so sodden irresolution and brutish inertia.

But this very tendency nourishes the germ of resistance that ripens into the spirit of revolt.

The labor movement is the child of slavery—the offspring of oppression—in revolt against the misery and suffering that gave it birth.

Its splendid growth is the marvel of our time, the forerunner of freedom, the hope of mankind.

Ten thousand times has the labor movement stumbled and fallen and bruised itself, and risen again; been seized by the throat and choked and clubbed into insensibility; enjoined by courts, assaulted by thugs, charged by the militia, shot down by regulars, traduced by the press, frowned upon by public opinion, deceived by politicians, threatened by priests, repudiated by renegades, preyed upon by grafters, infested by spies, deserted by cowards, betrayed by traitors, bled by leeches, and sold out by leaders, but, notwithstanding all this, and all these, it is today the most vital and potential power this planet has every known, and its historic mission of emancipating the workers of the world from the thraldom of the ages is as certain of ultimate realization as the setting of the sun.

The most vital thing about this world movement is its educational propaganda—its capacity and power to shed light in the brain of the working class, arouse them from their torpor, develop their faculties for thinking, teach them their economic class interests, effect their solidarity, and imbue them with the spirit of the impending social revolution.

In this propaganda the life-breath of the movement, the press, is paramount to all other agencies and influences, and the progress of the press a sure index of the progress of the movement.

Unfortunately, the workers lack intelligent appreciation of the importance of the press; they also lack judgment and discrimination in dealing with the subject, and utterly neglect some good papers, and permit them to perish, while others that are anything but helpful or beneficial to the cause they are supposed to represent are liberally patronized and flourish in the ignorance and stupidity which support them.

The material prosperity of a labor paper of today is no guarantee of its moral or intellectual value. Indeed, some of the most worthless labor publications have the finest mechanical appearance, and are supported by the largest circulations.

Such a press is not only not a help to labor but a millstone about its neck, that only the awakening intelligence of the working class can remove.

How thoroughly alive the capitalists are to the power of the press! And how assiduously they develop and support it that it may in turn buttress their class interests!

The press is one of their most valuable assets, and, as an investment, pays the highest dividends.

When there is trouble between capital and labor the press volleys and thunders against labor and its unions and leaders and all other things that dare to breathe against the sacred rights of capital. In such a contest labor is dumb, speechless; it has no press that reaches the public, and must submit to the vilest calumny, the most outrageous misrepresentation.

The lesson has been taught in all the languages of labor and written in the blood of its countless martyred victims.

Labor must have a press as formidable as the great movement of the working class requires, to worthily represent its dignity and fearlessly and uncompromisingly advocate its principles.

Every member of a trade union should feel himself obligated to do his full share in the important work of building up the press of the labor movement; he should at least support the paper of his union, and one or more of the papers of his party, and, above all, he should read them and school himself in the art of intelligent criticism, and let the editor hear from him when he has a criticism to offer or a suggestion to make.

The expense of supporting the labor press is but a trifle to the individual member—less than the president or any other officer of the union. He ought to be chosen with special reference to his knowledge upon the labor question and his fitness to advocate and defend the economic interests of the class he represents.

The vast amount of capitalist advertising some labor publications carry certifies unerringly to the worthlessness of their literary contents. Capitalists do not, as a rule, advertise in labor papers that are loyal to working class interests. It is only on condition that the advertising colors and controls the editorial that the capitalist generously allows his patronage to go to the labor paper.

The workingman who wants to read a labor paper with the true ring, one that ably, honestly and fearlessly speaks for the working class will find it safe to steer clear of those that are loaded with capitalist advertising and make his selection from those that are nearly or quite boycotted by the class that live and thrive upon the slavery and degradation of the working class.

The labor press of today is not ideal, but it is improving steadily, and the time will come when the ideal labor press will be realized; when the labor movement will command editors, writers, journalists, artists of the first class; when hundreds of papers, including dailies in the large cities, will gather the news and discuss it from the labor standpoint; when illustrated magazines and periodicals will illuminate the literature of labor and all will combine to realize our ideal labor press and blaze the way to victory.

The Metal Worker, May, 1904.

The crimson standard

A vast amount of ignorant prejudice prevails against the red flag. It is easily accounted for. The ruling class the wide world over hates it, and its sycophants, therefore must decry it.

Strange that the red flag should produce the same effect upon a tyrant that it does upon a bull.

The bull is enraged at the very sight of the red flag, his huge frame quivers, his eyes become balls of fire, and he paws the dirt and snorts with fury.

The reason for this peculiar effect of a bit of red coloring upon the bovine species we are not particularly interested in at this moment, but why does it happen to excite the same rage in the czar, the emperor and the king; the autocrat, the aristocrat and the plutocrat?

Ah, that is simple enough.

The red flag, since time immemorial, has symbolized the discontent of the downtrodden, the revolt of the rabble.

That is its sinister significance to the tyrant and the reason of his mingled fear and frenzy when the "red rag," as he characterizes it, insults his vision.

It is not that he is opposed to red as a color, or even as an emblem, for he has it in his own flags and banners, and it never inflames his passion when it is blended with other colors; but red alone, unmixed and unadulterated, the pure red that symbolizes the common blood of the human family, the equality of mankind, the brotherhood of the race, is repulsive and abhorrent to him because it is at once an impeachment of his title, a denial of his superiority and a menace to his power.

Precisely for the reason that the plutocrat raves at the red flag the proletaire should revere it.

To the plutocrat it is a peril; to the proletaire a promise.

The red flag is an omen of ill, a sign of terror to every tyrant, every robber and every vampire that sucks the life of labor and mocks at its misery.

It is an emblem of hope, a bow of promise to all the oppressed and downtrodden of the earth.

The red flag is the only race flag; it is the flag of revolt against robbery; the flag of the working class, the flag of hope and high resolve—the flag of Universal Freedom.

Appeal to Reason, 1905.

Revolutionary unionism

The unity of labor, economic and political, upon the basis of the class struggle, is at this time the supreme need of the working class. The prevailing lack of unity implies lack of class consciousness; that is to say, enlightened self-interest; and this can, must and will be overcome by revolutionary education and organization. Experience, long, painful and dearly bought, has taught some of us that craft division is fatal to class unity. To accomplish its mission the working class must be united. They must act together; they must assert their combined power, and when they do this upon the basis of the class struggle, then and then only will they break the fetters of wage slavery.

We are engaged today in a class war; and why? For the simple reason that in the evolution of the capitalist system in which we live, society has been mainly divided into two economic classes—a small class of capitalists who own the tools with which work is done and wealth is produced, and a great mass of workers who are compelled to use those tools. Between these two classes there is an irrepressible economic conflict. Unfortunately for himself, the workingman does not yet understand the nature of this conflict and for this reason has hitherto failed to accomplish any effective unity of his class.

It is true that workers in the various departments of industrial activity have organized trade unions. It is also true that in this capacity they have from time to time asserted such power as this form of organization has conferred upon them. It is equally true that mere craft unionism, no matter how well it may be organized, is in the present highly developed capitalist system utterly unable to successfully cope with the capitalist class. The old craft union has done its work and belongs to the past. Labor unionism, like everything else, must recognize and bow to the inexorable law of evolution.

The craft union says that the worker shall receive a fair day's pay for a fair day's work. What is a fair day's pay for a fair day's work? Ask the capitalist and he will give you his idea about it. Ask the worker and, if he is intelligent, he will tell you that a fair day's pay for a fair day's work is all the workingman produces.

While the craft unionist still talks about a fair day's pay for a fair day's work, implying that the economic interests of the capitalist and the worker can be harmonized upon a basis of equal justice to both, the Industrial Worker says, "I want all I produce by my labor."

If the worker is not entitled to all he produces, then what share is anybody else entitled to?

Does the worker today receive all he produces? Does he receive anything like a fair (?) share of the product of his labor? Will any trade-unionist of the old school make any such claim, and if he is bold enough to make it, can he verify it?

The student of this question knows that, as a matter of fact, in the capitalist system in which we live today the worker who produces all wealth receives but enough of his product to keep him in working and producing order. His wage, in the aggregate, is fixed by his living necessities. It suffices, upon the average, to maintain him according to the prevailing standard of living and to enable him to reproduce himself in the form of labor power. He receives, as a matter of fact, but about 17 percent of what his labor produces.

The worker produces a certain thing. It goes from the manufacturer to the jobber, from the jobber to the wholesaler, and from the wholesaler to the retailer—each of these adding a profit, and when it completes the circle and comes back to the worker who produced it and he stands face to face with the product of his own labor, he can buy back, upon the average, with his paltry wage but about 17 percent of it. In other words, he is exploited, robbed, of about 83 percent of what his labor produces. And why? For the simple reason that in modern industry, the tool, in the form of a great machine with which he works and produces, is the private property of the capitalist, who didn't make it, and could not if his life depended upon it, use it.

The evolution is not yet complete.

By virtue of his private ownership of the social tool—made and used by the co-operative labor of the working class—the employer has the economic power to appropriate to himself, as a capitalist, what is produced by the social labor of the working class. This accounts for the fact that the capitalist becomes fabulously rich, lives in a palace where there is music and singing and dancing, and where there is the luxury of all climes, while the workingmen who do the work and produce the wealth and endure the privations and make the sacrifices of health and limb and life, remain in a wretched state of poverty and dependence.

The exploiting capitalist is the economic master and the political ruler in capitalist society, and as such holds the exploited wage worker in utter contempt.

No master ever had any respect for his slave, and no slave ever had, or ever could have, any real love for his master.

I must beg you to indulge the hoarseness of my voice, which has been somewhat strained addressing meetings of the Industrial Workers held in and about Chicago during the last two or three evenings; but, fortunately, my eyesight has not been strained reading the accounts of these meetings in the capitalists papers of Chicago.

Alert, vigilant, argus-eyed as the capitalist dailies of Chicago are, there is not one of them that knows of this meeting of the Industrial Workers. But if this were a meeting of the American Federation of Labor and an old trade union leader were here, you would read tomorrow morning a full account of it and him in every capitalist paper in the city. There is a reason for this that explains itself.

The capitalist papers know that there is such an organization as the Industrial Workers, because they have lied about it. Just now they are ignoring it. Let me serve notice on them through you and the thousands of others who flock to our meetings everywhere, that they will reckon with the Industrial Workers before six months have rolled around.

There are those wage workers who feel their economic dependence, who know that the capitalist for whom they work is the owner of their job, and therefore the master of their fate, who are still vainly seeking by individual effort and through waning craft unions to harmonize the conflicting interests of the exploiting capitalist and the exploited wage slave. They are engaged in a vain and hopeless task. They are wasting time and energy worthy of a better cause. These interests never can and never will be harmonized permanently, and when they are adjusted even temporarily it is always at the expense of the working class.

I t is no part of the mission of this revolutionary working class union to conciliate the capitalist class. We are organized to fight that class, and we want that class to distinctly understand it. And they do understand it, and in time the working class will also understand it; and then the capitalist class will have reason to understand it better still. Their newspapers understand it so well even now that they have not a single favorable comment to make upon it.

When the convention of delegates was in session here in June last for the purpose of organizing the Industrial Workers, every report that appeared in a Chicago paper—capitalist paper I mean; every single report was a tissue of perversion, misstatement and downright falsehood. They knew that we had met for a purpose, and that that purpose was to fight the class of which they are the official mouthpieces. Now, it seems to me that this uniform hostility of the capitalist press ought to be significant to even the unthinking workingman. Capitalist papers are, as a rule, quite friendly to the craft unions. They do not misrepresent them; do not lie about them; do not traduce their representatives. They are exceedingly fond of them, because they know enough about their own interests to know that the craft unions are not a menace to them, but are in fact bulwarks of defense to them. And why? Because, chiefly, craft unions divide and do not unite the working class. And I challenge contradiction.

There was a time when the craft union expressed in terms of unionism the prevailing mode of industry. That was long ago when production was still mainly carried on by handicraftmen with hand tools; when one man worked for another to learn his trade that he might become its master. The various trades involved skill and cunning; considerable time was required to master them. This was in the early stages of the capitalist system. Even at that early day the antagonism between employer and employed found expression, although the employer was not at that time the capitalist as he is today. The men who followed these trades found it necessary in order to protect themselves in their trade interests to band together, form a union, so that they might act together in resisting the encroachments of the "boss." So the trade union came into existence.

The mode of production since that time has been practically revolutionized. The hand tool has all but disappeared. The mammoth machine has taken its place. The hand tool was made and used by the individual worker and was largely within his own control. Today the machine that has supplanted the old tool is not owned or controlled by the man, or rather the men, who use it. As I have already said, it is the private property of some capitalist who may live at a remote point and never have seen the machine or the wage slaves who operate it.

In other words, the production of wealth, in the evolution of industry, from being an individual act a half a century ago has become a social act. The tool, from being an individual tool, has become a social instrument. So that the tool has been socialized and production has also been socialized. But the evolution is yet to complete its work. This social tool, made socially and used socially, must be socially owned.

In the evolution of industry the trade has been largely undermined. The old trade union expresses the old form of industry, the old mode of individual production based upon the use of the individual tool. That tool has about disappeared; that mode of production has also about disappeared, but the trade union built upon that mode of production, springing from the use of the hand tool, remains essentially the same.

The pure and simple trade union, in seeking to preserve its autonomy, is forced into conflict with other trade unions by the unceasing operation of the laws of industrial evolution. How many of the skilled trades that were in operation half a century ago are still practiced?

At the town where I live there used to be quite a number of cooper shops. Barrels were made by hand and a cooper shop consisted wholly of coopers. The coopers' union was organized and served fairly well the purposes of the coopers of that day, but it does not serve the purposes of the workers who make barrels today. They do not make barrels in the way they used to be made. Today we want a union that expresses the economic interests of all the workers in the cooperage plant engaged in making and handling barrels. But a few coopers still remain, a very few. It is no longer necessary to be a cooper to make a barrel. The machine is the cooper today. The machine makes the barrel, and almost anyone can operate the machine that makes the barrel.

You will observe that labor has been subdivided and specialized and that the trade has been dissipated; and now a body of men and boys work together co-operatively in the making of a barrel, each making a small part of a barrel. Now we want a union which embraces all the workers engaged in making barrels. We lose sight of the cooper trade as evolution has practically disposed of that. We say that since the trade has completely changed, the union which expressed that trade must also change accordingly. In the new union we shall include not only the men who are actually engaged in the making of barrels directly, but also those who are placing them upon the market. There are the typewriters, the bookkeepers, the teamsters, and all other classes of labor that are involved in the making and delivering of the barrels. We insist that all the workers in the whole of any given plant shall belong to one and the same union.

This is the very thing the workers need and the capitalist who owns the establishment does not want. He believes in labor unionism if it is the "right kind." And if it is the right kind for him it is the wrong kind for you. He is more than willing that his employees shall join the craft union. He has not the slightest objection. On the contrary, it is easily proven that capitalists are among the most active upholders of the old craft union.

The capitalists are perfectly willing that you shall organize, as long as you don't do a thing against them; as long as you don't do a thing for yourselves. You cannot do a thing for yourselves without antagonizing them; and you don't antagonize them through your craft unions nearly as much as you buttress their interests and prolong their mastery.

The average workingman imagines that he must have a leader to look to; a guide to follow, right or wrong. He has been taught in the craft union that he is a very dependent creature; that without a leader the goblins would get him without a doubt, and he therefore instinctively looks to his leader. And even while he is looking at his leader there is someone else looking at the same leader from the other side.

You have depended too much on that leader and not enough on yourself. I don't want you to follow me. I want you to cultivate self-reliance.

If I have the slightest capacity for leadership I can only give evidence of it by leading you to rely upon yourselves.

As long as you can be led by an individual you will be betrayed by an individual. That does not mean that all leaders are dishonest or corrupt. I make no such sweeping indictment. I know that many of them are honest. I know also that many of them are in darkness themselves, blind leaders of the blind. That is the worst that can be said of them. And let me say to you that the most dangerous leader is not the corrupt leader, but the honest, ignorant leader. That leader is just as fatal to your interests as the one who deliberately sells you out for a paltry consideration.

You are a workingman! Now, at your earliest leisure look your-self over and take an inventory of your resources. Invoice your mental stock; see what you have on hand.

You may be of limited mentality; and that is all you require in the capitalist system. You need only small brains, but huge hands.

Most of your hands are calloused and you are taught by the capitalist politician, who is the political mercenary of the capitalist who fleeces you, you are taught by him to be proud of your horny hands. If that is true he ought to be ashamed of his. He doesn't have any horns on his hands. He has them on his brains. He is as busy with his brain as you are with your hands, and because he is busy with his brain and you neglect yours, he gets a goodly share of what you produce with your hands. He is the gentleman who calls you the horny handed sons of toil. That fetches you every time. I tell you that the time has come for you to use your brains in your own interest, and until you do that you will have to use your hands in the interest of your masters.

Now, after you have looked yourself over; after you have satisfied yourself what you are, or rather, what you are not, you will arrive at the conclusion that as a wage worker in capitalist society you are not a man at all. You are simply a thing. And that thing is bought in the labor market, just as hair, hides and other forms of merchandise are bought.

When the capitalist requires the use of your hands, does he call for men? Why, certainly not. He doesn't want men, he only wants hands. And when he calls for hands, that is what he wants. Have you ever seen a placard posted: "Fifty hands wanted"? Did you ever know of a capitalist to respond to that kind of an invitation?

President Roosevelt would have you believe that there are no classes in the United States. He was made president by the votes of the working class. Did you ever know of his stopping over night in the home of a workingman? Is it by mere chance that he is always sheltered beneath the hospitable roof of some plutocrat? Not long ago he made a visit here and he gave a committee representing the workers about fifteen minutes of his precious time, just time enough to rebuke them with the intimation that organized labor consisted of a set of law-breakers, and then he gave fifteen hours to the plutocrats of Chicago, being wined and dined by them to prove that there are no classes in the United States, and that you, horny handed veteran, with your wage of $1.50 a day, with six children to support on that, are in the same class with John D. Rockefeller! Your misfortune is that you do not know you are in the same class. But on election day it dawns upon you and you prove it by voting the same ticket.

Since you have looked yourself over thoroughly, you realize by this time that, as a workingman, you have been supporting, through your craft unions and through your ballots, a social system that is the negation of your manhood.

The capitalist for whom you work doesn't have to go out and look for you; you have to look for him, and you belong to him just as completely as if he had a title to your body; as if you were his chattel slave.

He doesn't own you under the law, but he does under the fact.

Why? Because he owns the tool with which you work, and you have got to have access to that tool if you work; and if you eat; and so, scourged by hunger pangs, you look about for that tool and you locate it, and you soon discover that between yourself, a working-man, and that tool that is an essential part of yourself in industry, there stands the capitalist who owns it. He is your boss; he owns your job, takes your product and controls your destiny. Before you can touch that tool to earn a dime you must petition the owner of it to allow you to use it, in consideration of your giving to him all you produce with it, except just enough to keep you alive and in working order.

Observe that you are displaced by the surplus product of your own labor; that what you produce is of more value under capitalism than you who produce it; that the commodity which is the result of your labor is of greater value under capitalism than your own life. You consist of palpitating flesh; you have wants. You have necessities. You cannot satisfy them, and you suffer. But the product of your labor, the property of the capitalist, that is sacred; that must be protected at all hazards. After you have been displaced by the surplus product of your labor and you have been idle long enough, you become restive and you begin to speak out, and you become a menace. The unrest culminates in trouble. The capitalist presses a button and the police are called into action. Then the capitalist presses button No. 2 and injunctions are issued by the judges, the judicial allies and servants of the capitalist class. Then button No. 3 is pressed and the state troops fall into line; and if this is not sufficient button No. 4 is pressed and the regular soldiers come marching to the scene. That is what President Roosevelt meant when he said that back of the mayor is the governor; back of the governor, the President; or, to use his own words, back of the city, the state, and back of the state the nation—the capitalist nation.

If you have been working in a steel mill and you have made more steel than your master can sell, and you are locked out and get hungry, and the soldiers are called out, it is to protect the steel and shoot you who made the steel—to guard the men who steal the steel and kill the men who made it.

I am not asking you to withdraw from the craft unions simply because the Industrial Workers has been formed. I am asking you to think about these matters for yourselves.

I belonged to a craft union from the time I was nineteen years of age. I can remember the very evening I first joined the Brotherhood of Locomotive Firemen. I can recall with what zeal I went to work to organize my craft, and it was the pride of my life to see that union expand. I did what I could to build it up. In time I was made to realize that that union was not sufficient unto itself. I next did what I could to organize other branches of the service and then establish a federation of the various unions of railroad employees, and finally succeeded; but soon after the federation was formed, on account of craft jealousies, it was disrupted. I then, along with a number of others who had had the same experience and had profited by it, undertook to organize the railway men within one organization, known as the American Railway Union. The railroad corporations were the deadly enemies of that organization. They understood that its purpose was to unify all the railroad employees. They knew that the unity of the working class meant their end, and so they set their faces like flint against the American Railway Union. And while they were using all their powers to crush and to stamp out the American Railway Union, they were bestowing all their favors upon the several craft brotherhoods, the engineers and the firemen, the conductors and the brakemen. They knew that so long as these craft unions existed there could be no unification of the men employed in the railway service.

Revolutionary unionism

Are the railroad men of this country organized today? No! Not nearly one-half of them are organized at all. And when the railroad corporations from motives of good policy make a concession to the engineers or the conductors, it is gouged out of the poor devils who work for a dollar a day and are compelled to submit.

There are great many engineers who are perfectly willing to be tied up in a contract. They think they can save themselves at the expense of their fellow-workers. But they are going to reap, sooner or later, just what they have sown. In the next few years they will become motormen.

While we are upon this question, let us consult industrial history a moment. We will begin with the craft union railroad strike of 1888. The Brotherhood of Engineers and the Brotherhood of Firemen on the C., B. & Q. system went out on strike. Some 2,000 engineers and firemen vacated their posts and went out on one of the most bitterly contested railroad strikes in the history of the country. When they went out, the rest of the employees, especially the conductors, who were organized in craft unions of their own, remained at their posts, and the union conductors piloted the scab engineers over the line. I know whereof I speak. I was there. I took an active part in that strike.

I saw craft union pitted against craft union, and I saw the Brotherhood of Engineers and the Brotherhood of Firemen completely wiped from the C., B. & Q. system. And now you find these men, seventeen years later, scattered all over the United States. They had to pay the penalty of their ignorance in organizing a craft instead of organizing as a whole.

In 1892 a strike occurred on the Lehigh Valley; the same result. Another on the Toledo, Ann Arbor & North Michigan. Same result. The engineers have had no strike from that time to this. Every time they have had a strike they have been defeated.

The railroad corporations are shrewd enough to recognize the fact that if they can keep certain departments in their employ in a time of emergency they can defeat all of the rest. A manager of a railroad who can keep control of 15 percent of the old men can allow 85 percent to go out on strike and defeat them every time. That is why they have made some concessions to the engineers and conductors and brakemen, and now and then to the switchmen, the most militant labor union of them all.

A year and a half ago the telegraph operators on the Missouri, Kansas & Texas went out on strike. The engineer remained at his post; so did the fireman; the conductor at his; and the brakeman at his. And they hauled the scabs that flocked from all parts of the country to the several points along the line, and delivered them in good order to take the places vacated by the strikers; worked all round them and with them until they had mastered the details of their several duties; and having done this, the strike was at an end, and the 1,300 craft unionists out of jobs. You will find them scattered all over the country.

Now, were not these other craft unions scabbing on the telegraphers just as flagrantly as if they had stepped into their position and discharged their duties? They were acting with the corporation against their union fellow workingmen, helping the corporation to defeat and crush them. Without their aid the corporation could not have succeeded. With their aid it was very easily done.

Is it possible that a craft unionist can see such an object lesson as this so plainly presented to him and still refuse to profit by it? Still close his eyes and, as it were, shut up his reason, and absolutely decline to see that this is suicidal policy and that its fruit must always be disruption and disaster?

This world only respects as it is compelled to respect; and if you workingmen would be respected you must begin by respecting yourselves. You have had enough of this sort of experience. You have had more than enough of it right here in Chicago.

Why didn't the steel trust annihilate the Amalgamated Steelworkers? Only two years ago they defeated them completely. The trust had its iron heel upon the neck of the Steelworkers' Union, and could have, had it chosen, completely crushed the life out of it. But Morgan was too wily. Schwab was too wise. They used to oppose trade unions. They don't oppose them any longer. They have discovered that a union can be turned the other way; that it can be made useful to them instead of being useful to the working class. Morgan now says he is in favor of trade unions, and Schwab agrees. They didn't crush out the Steelworkers' Union because they knew that another and a better one would spring from its ruins. They were perfectly willing that the old craft union should grow up again and block the way to real union.

You have had the machinists' strike here in Chicago. You are well aware of this without my telling you. There is something pathetic to me about every strike.

I have said and say again that no strike was ever lost; that it has always been worth all it cost. An essential part of a workingman's education is the defeats he encounters. The strikes he loses are after all the only ones he wins. I am heartily glad for myself that I lost the strike. It is the best thing that ever happened to me. I lost the strike of the past that I may win the strike of the future.

I am a discredited labor leader, but I have good staying qualities. The very moment the capitalist press credits me with being a wise labor leader, I will invite you to investigate me upon the charge of treason. I am discredited by the capitalist simply because I am true to his victim. I don't want his favors. I do not court his approbation. I would not have it. I can't afford it. If I had this respect it would be at the price of my own.

I don't care anything about what is called public opinion. I know precisely what that means. It is but the reflection of the interests of the capitalists class. As between the respect of the public and my own, I prefer my own; and I am going to keep it until I can have both.

When I pick up a capitalist newspaper and read a eulogy of some labor leader, I know that that leader has at least two afflictions; the one is mental weakness and the other is moral cowardice—and they go together. Put it down that when the capitalist who is exploiting you credits your leader with being safe and conservative and wise, that leader is not serving you. And if you take exception to that statement, just ask me to prove it.

The rank and file of all unions, barring their ignorance, are all right. The working class as a whole is all right. Many of them are misguided, and stand in the light of their own interest.

It is sometimes necessary that we offend you and even shock you, that you may understand that we are your friends and not your enemies. And if we are against your unions it is because we are for you. We know that you have paid your dues into them for years and that you are animated by a spirit of misdirected loyalty to those unions.

I can remember that it was not a very easy matter for me to give up the union in which I had spent my boyhood and all the years of my young manhood. I remember that I felt there was something in it in the nature of a sacrifice, and yet I had to make it in the interest of the larger duty that I owed myself and the working class.

Let me say to you, if you are a craft unionist, that infinitely greater than your loyalty to your craft is your loyalty to the working class as a whole. No craft union can fight this great battle successfully alone. The craft is a part, a part only, of the great body of the working class. And the time has come for this class, numerically overwhelmingly in the majority, to follow in one respect at least the example of its capitalist masters and unite as a whole.

In this barbarous competitive struggle in which we are engaged, the workers, the millions, are fighting each other to sell themselves into slavery; the middle class are fighting each other to get enough trade to keep soul and body together, and the professional class are fighting each other like savages for practice. And this is called civilization! What a mockery! What a sham! There is no real civilization in the capitalist system.

Today there is nothing so easily produced as wealth. The whole earth consists of raw materials; and in every breath of nature, in sunshine, and in shower, hidden everywhere, are the subtle forces that may, by the touch of the hand of labor, be set into operation to transmute these raw materials into wealth, the finished products, in all their multiplied forms and in opulent abundance for all. The merest child can press a button that will set in operation a forest of machinery and produce wealth enough for a community.

Whatever may be said of the ignorant, barbarous past, there is no excuse for poverty today. And yet it is the scourge of the race. It is the Nemesis of capitalist civilization. Ten millions, one-eighths of our whole population, are in a state of chronic poverty. Three millions of these have been sunk to unresisting pauperism. The whole working class is in a sadly dependent state, and even the most favored wage-worker is left suspended by a single thread. He does not know what hour a machine may be invented to make his trade useless, displace him and throw him into the increasing army of the unemployed.

And how does labor live today? Here in Chicago you may walk along a certain boulevard, say 18th street, and you will find it lined with magnificent palaces. Beyond that you will find a larger district where the still complacent middle class abide. Beyond that is a very much larger territory where the working class exists; and still beyond

---

that, to complete the circle, you see the red lights flickering in the distance.

Prostitution is a part, a necessary part, of capitalist society. The department store empties in the slums.

I have been here enough to know that when the daughter of a workingman is obliged to go up the street to look for employment, when she is fourteen or fifteen years of age, and ought to be in the care and keeping of a loving mother, and have all of the advantages that our civilization makes possible for all—when she is forced to go to a department store, to one of those capitalist emporiums, and there find a place, if she can, and work for a wage of $3 a week, and have to obey a code of cast-iron regulations, appear tidy and neatly dressed and be subject to a thousand temptations daily, and then takes a mis-step, the first, as she is more than apt to do, especially if she has no home in any decent sense of that term—the very instant this is added to her poverty, she is doomed—damned. All the doors of capitalist society are closed in her face. The coals of contumely are poured upon her head. There is for her no redemption, and she takes the next step, and the next, until at last she ends a disgraceful career in a brothel hell.

This may be your child. And if you are a workingman, and this should fall to the lot of the innocent blue-eyed child that you love more than you do your own life—I want you to realize that if such a horror be written in the book of fate, that you are responsible for it, if you use or misuse your power to perpetuate the capitalist system and working class slavery.

You can change this condition—not tomorrow, not next week, nor next year; but in the meantime the next thing to changing it is making up your mind that it shall be changed. That is what we Industrial Unionists have done. And so there has come to us a new state of mind, and in our hearts there is the joy of service and the serenity of triumph.

We are united and we cannot be disunited. We cannot be stampeded. We know that we are confronted by ten thousand difficulties. We know that all the powers of capitalism are to be arrayed against us. But were these obstacles multiplied by a million, it would simply have the effect of multiplying our determination by a million, to overcome them all. And so we are organizing and appealing to you.

The workingman today does not understand his industrial relation to his fellow-workers. He has never been correlated with others in the same industry. He has mechanically done his part. He has simply been a cog, with little reference to, or knowledge of, the rest of the cogs. Now, we teach him to hold up his head and look over the whole mechanism. If he is employed in a certain plant, as an Industrial Unionist, his eyes are opened. He takes a survey of the entire productive mechanism, and he understands his part in it, and his relation to every other worker in that industry. The very instant he does that he is buoyed by a fresh hope and thrilled with a new aspiration. He becomes a larger man. He begins to feel like a collective son of toil.

Then he and his fellows study to fit themselves to take control of this productive mechanism when it shall be transferred from the idle capitalist to the workers to whom it rightfully belongs.

In every mill and every factory, every mine and every quarry, every railroad and every shop, everywhere, the workers, enlightened, understanding their self-interest, are correlating themselves in the industrial and economic mechanism. They are developing their industrial consciousness, their economic and political power; and when the revolution comes, they will be prepared to take possession and assume control of every industry. With the education they will have received in the Industrial Workers they will be drilled and disciplined, trained and fitted for Industrial Mastery and Social Freedom.

Speech at Chicago, November 25, 1905.

John Brown:
History's greatest hero

The most picturesque character, the bravest man and most self-sacrificing soul in American history, was hanged at Charleston, Va., December 2, 1859.

On that day Thoreau said: "Some eighteen hundred years ago Christ was crucified. This morning, perchance, Captain Brown was hung. These are the two ends of a chain which is not without its links. He is not 'Old Brown' any longer; he is an Angel of Light. ...I foresee the time when the painter will paint the scene, no longer going to Rome for a subject; the poet will sing it, the historian record it, and with the landing of the Pilgrims and the Declaration of Independence it will be the ornament of some future national gallery, when at least the present form of slavery shall be no more here. We shall then be at liberty to weep for Captain Brown."

Few people dared on that fateful day to breathe a sympathetic word for the grizzled old agitator. For years he had carried on his warfare against chattel slavery. He had only a handful of fanatical followers to support him. But to his mind his duty was clear, and that was enough. He would fight it out to the end, and if need be alone.

Old John Brown set an example of moral courage and of single-hearted devotion to an idea for all men and for all ages.

With every drop of his honest blood he hated slavery, and in his early manhood he resolved to lay his life on Freedom's altar in wiping out that insufferable affliction. He never faltered. So God-like was his unconquerable soul that he dared to face the world alone.

How perfectly sublime!

He did not reckon the overwhelming numbers against him, nor the paltry few that were on his side. This grosser aspect of the issue found no lodgment in his mind or heart. He was right and Jehovah was with him. His was not to reckon consequences, but to strike the immortal blow and step from the gallows to the throne of God.

Not for earthly glory did John Brown wage his holy warfare; not for any recognition or reward the people had it in their power to bestow. His great heart was set upon a higher goal, animated by a loftier ambition. His grand soul was illuminated by a sublimer ideal.

A race of human beings, lowly and despised, were in chains, and this festering crime was eating out the heart of civilization.

In the presence of this awful plague logic was silent, reason dumb, pity dead.

The wrath of retributive justice, long asleep, awakened at last and hurled its lurid bolt. Old John Brown struck the blow and the storm broke. That hour chattel slavery was dead.

In the first frightful convulsion the slave power seized the grand old liberator by the throat, put him in irons and threw him into a dungeon to await execution.

Alas! it was too late. His work was done. All Virginia could do was to furnish the crown for his martyrdom.

Victor Hugo exclaimed in a burst of reverential passion: "John Brown is grander than George Washington!"

History may be searched in vain for an example of noble heroism and sublime self-sacrifice equal to that of Old John Brown.

From the beginning of his career to its close he had but one idea and one ideal, and that was to destroy chattel slavery; and in that cause he sealed his devotion with his noble blood. Realizing that his work was done, he passed serenely, almost with joy, from the scenes of men.

His calmness upon the gallows was awe-inspiring; his exaltation supreme.

Old John Brown is not dead. His soul still marches on, and each passing year weaves new garlands for his brow and adds fresh lustre to his deathless glory.

Who shall be the John Brown of Wage-Slavery?

Appeal to Reason, November 23, 1907.

Mother Jones

"**T**he 'Grand Old Woman' of the revolutionary movement" is the appropriate title given to Mother Jones by Walter Hurt. All who know her—and they are legion—will at once recognize the fitness of the title.

The career of this unique old agitator reads like romance. There is no other that can be compared to it. For fifteen years she has been at the forefront, and never once has she been known to flinch.

From the time of the Pullman strike in 1894, when she first came into prominence, she has been steadily in the public eye. With no desire to wear "distinction's worthless badge," utterly forgetful of self and scorning of selfish ambitions, this brave woman has fought the battles of the oppressed with a heroism more exalted than ever sustained a soldier upon the field of carnage.

Mother Jones is not one of the "summer soldiers" or "sunshine patriots." Her pulses burn with true patriotic fervor, and whenever the battle waxes hottest there she surely will be found upon the firing line.

For many weary months at a time has she lived amid the most desolate regions of West Virginia, organizing the half-starved miners, making her home in their wretched cabins, sharing her meager substance with their families, nursing the sick and cheering the disconsolate—a true minister of mercy.

During the great strike in the anthracite coal district she marched at the head of the miners; was first to meet the sheriff and the soldiers, and last to leave the field of battle.

Again and again has this dauntless soul been driven out of some community by corporation hirelings, enjoined by courts, locked up in jail, prodded by the bayonets of soldiers, and threatened with assassination. But never once in all her self-surrendering life has she shown the white feather; never once given a single sign of weakness or discouragement. In the Colorado strikes Mother Jones was feared, as was no other, by the criminal corporations; feared by them as she was loved by the sturdy miners she led again and again in the face of overwhelming odds until, like Henry of Navarre, where her snow-white crown was seen, the despairing slaves took fresh courage and fought again with all their waning strength against the embattled foe.

Deported at the point of bayonets, she bore herself so true a warrior that she won even the admiration of the soldiers, whose order it was to escort her to the boundary lines and guard against her return.

No other soldier in the revolutionary cause has a better right to recognition in this edition than has Mother Jones.

Her very name expresses the Spirit of the Revolution.

Her striking personality embodies all its principles.

She has won her way into the hearts of the nation's toilers, and her name is revered at the altars of their humble firesides and will be lovingly remembered by their children and their children's children forever.

Appeal to Reason, November 23, 1907.

Thomas McGrady

It is a strange and pathetic coincidence that almost at the very moment I completed the introduction to the brochure of Thomas McGrady on "The Catholic Church and Socialism," now in press, the sad news came that he had passed away, and the painful duty now devolves upon me to write the word "finis" at the close of his work and add a few words of obitual eulogy.

It is not customary among Socialists to pronounce conventional and meaningless panegyrics upon departed comrades; nor to pay fulsome tribute to virtues they never possessed. Mere form and ceremony have had their day—and a long and gloomy day it has been—and can have no place among Socialists when a comrade living pays his last reverent regards to a comrade dead.

Thomas McGrady was born at Lexington, Ky., June 6, 1863. In 1887, at 24 years of age, he was ordained as a Catholic priest at the Cathedral of Galveston, Tex. His next pastorate was St. Patrick's church, Houston, followed by his transfer to St. Patrick's church, Dallas, Tex. In 1890 he returned to his Kentucky home, beginning his pastoral service there in Lexington, his native city. Later he went to St. Anthony's church, Bellevue, Ky., and it was here, in 1896, that he began his first serious study of economic, political and social questions. He was first attracted by Henry George's Single Tax, but abandoned that as inadequate after some Socialist literature fell into his hands, and he became convinced that nothing less than a social revolution, and the abolition of the capitalist competitive system would materially better the existing industrial and social condition of the people.

Father McGrady, who always had the lofty courage of his convictions, now avowed himself a Socialist. He drank deep at the fountain of Socialist literature and mastered its classics. His library contained the works of the standard authors of all nations.

It was at this time that Father McGrady was at the very pinnacle of his priestly power and popularity. He was young, just past thirty, and brilliant and scholarly. His magnetic personality was irresistible. Tall, fully six feet, splendidly proportioned, commanding, he was a magnificent specimen of physical manhood. He had a massive head, a full, fine face, florid complexion, clear features, and the bluest, kindliest and most expressive of eyes.

Widely and deeply read, cultured in the genuine sense, sociable and sympathetic, Father McGrady attracted friends by an irresistible charm, and held them by the same magic power.

He was an orator, and a wit, a scholar and a humanitarian.

He had the exquisite fancy of a poet and could dally, according to mood, with a daisy or a star.

In his heroic and finely moulded physical proportions, his large and shapely head, clear complexion and expressive eyes, he resembled strongly Robert G. Ingersoll.

This resemblance was accentuated by the kindly and infectious humor, the brilliant flashes of wit, the terse and epigrammatic speech, and the keen and incisive satire of which both were master.

These two men, had they not been separated by the cruel and hateful prejudices inherent in capitalist society, and all its conventional institutions, would have been the boonest of friends and loved each other as brothers.

Father McGrady soon began to feel that his new convictions did not fit his old conventicle. Honesty and candor being his predominant characteristics, the truth that dawned upon his brain found ready expression from his eloquent lips. He took his congregation into his confidence and told them frankly that he was a Socialist. Thenceforward every discourse attested that fact. He was warned by the bishop, threatened by the archbishop, but his flock closed around him, a living, throbbing citadel. He ministered to them in their suffering, comforted them in their sorrow, solemnized their nuptial vows, baptized their babes, tenderly laid to rest their dead, and they truly loved him.

But the conviction that the orthodox pulpit and the forum of freedom were irreconcilable, and that as a priest he was in the fetters of theology, grew upon him, and in spite of the pleadings and protesting of his followers he resigned his pastorate and withdrew from the priesthood. The touching scene attending his farewell sermon has never been described, and never will be, in human speech. The congregation, seeming more like one great family, under Father McGrady's tender and affectionate ministrations, felt stricken as if by an unspeakably sad personal bereavement, and sat in silence as they paid homage to their departing friend and pastor in sobs and tears.

The tremendous public reception given the modern Saul at Cincinnati, across the Ohio from his Kentucky home, is vividly remembered by thousands who struggled in the crush of common humanity to get within sound of his voice. He was now a full-fledged Social Revolutionist, and like his immortal prototype of many centuries ago, the common people heard him gladly.

The formal abdication of the priesthood by Father McGrady created a great sensation. The dignitaries of the church affected pious rejoicing. The recreant priest had long been a thorn in their complacent flesh. It was well that the holy church was purged of his pernicious influence.

Columns of reports appeared in the daily papers, and the features of the converted priest, with which these accounts were embellished became familiar to hundreds of thousands. A Socialist priest was indeed an anomaly. Vast concourses of people were attracted by the mere mention of his name. When he was announced to speak, standing room was always at a premium.

McGrady was now at his best. The deep convictions he was now free to express flowered in his speech and his oratory, like the peals of a great organ and the chimes of sweet bells, moved and swayed the eager masses. Everywhere the eloquent exponent of Socialism and pleader for the oppressed was in demand. His fame preceded his footsteps. Auditoriums, theaters and public halls were taxed to their capacity. The eloquent Socialist evangelist was now one of the commanding figures of the American platform. He was doing, superbly doing, the grand work for which he had been fitted as if by special providence. From the Atlantic seaboard to the Pacific slope his resonant voice was heard and the multitude were stirred by his burning message of social regeneration.

It was in the midst of these oratorical triumphs that the first distinct shock of organized opposition was felt. The capitalist press as a unit, and as if by preconcerted action, cut him out of its columns. The sensation created by McGrady's leap from the Catholic pulpit to the Socialist platform had been fully exploited as far as its news value was concerned, and now the renegade priest, as his whilom paters in Christ, who profess to love their enemies, call him, must be relegated to oblivion by being totally ignored. The church he formerly served so faithfully now began to actively pursue him. Where he was announced to speak priests admonished the faithful, either openly from the pulpit or covertly through the confessional, not to stain their souls by venturing near the anti-Christ. But this form of opposition, however vexatious, trying and difficult to overcome, but aroused the latent spirit of the crusader and intensified his determination. In the fierce fires of persecution, fed and fanned by religious ignorance and fanaticism, he was tempered for the far greater work that spread out before him, rich and radiant as a field of promise.

"Unhappy man!" as Hugo wrote of Marshal Ney, who bared his breast to the leaden hail of English foe on the field of Waterloo, "Thou wast reserved for French bullets!"

Notwithstanding that McGrady was attracting vast audiences, including many who had never before heard the philosophy of Socialism expounded, the very ones most desired, and without whom progress is impossible; notwithstanding the door receipts almost uniformly recouped the treasury of the local Socialists by a substantial net balance, certain "leaders," whose narrow prejudices were inflamed by the new agitator's success and increasing popularity in the movement, began to turn upon him, and sting him with venomous innuendo or attack him openly through the Socialist press.

Paradoxical as it may seem, he was denied the right to serve the Socialist movement—by Socialists.

Among the first charges brought against him—not by capitalists; they were too wise, if not too decent, to utter such a palpable untruth, but by men calling themselves Socialists—was that he had joined the movement as a "grafter," and was making Socialist speeches for "the money there was in it."

A baser falsehood, a more atrocious slander was never uttered.

Had McGrady been a miserable grafter instead of a great white soul, he would have remained in the pulpit. His people worshipped him and his "superiors" held out the most glittering inducements if he would only abandon his wicked and abominable "economic heresies." The eloquence and power of the young priest were widely recognized in church circles. A brilliant future spread out before him. He could easily become the petted and pampered favorite of the fathers. But he spurned the life of ease and luxury at the price of his self-respect. The positions of eminence he might attain by stifling his convictions sank to degradation from his lofty point of view.

Turning his back upon the wealth and luxury of the capitalist class he cast his lot with the proletariat, the homeless and hungry, the ragged and distressed, and this he did, according to some Socialists, to "graft" on them, and the cry was raised, "The grafter must go!"

It was this that shocked his tender sensibilities, silenced his eloquent tongue, and broke his noble and generous heart.

Those Socialists who vilified him as a "sky pilot," and as a "grafter," who declared him to be "unsound," "unscientific," and who indulged in similar tirade and twaddle, ought now to be satisfied. Their ambition has been realized. They scourged the "fakir" from the platform with whips of asps into a premature grave and he will trouble them no more. May they find it in their consciences to forgive themselves.

There is a deep lesson in the melancholy and untimely death of Comrade Thomas McGrady. Let us hope that so much good may result from it that the cruel sacrifice may be softened by the atonement and serve the future as a noble and inspiring example.

While it is the duty of every member to guard the movement against the impostor, the chronic suspicion that a man who has risen above the mental plane of a scavenger is a "grafter" is a besetting sin, and has done incalculable harm to the movement. The increasing cry from the same source that only the proletariat is revolutionary and that "intellectuals" are middle class reactionaries is an insult to the movement, many of whose staunchest supporters are of the latter type. Moreover, it would imply by its sneering allusion to the "intellectuals" that the proletariat are a brainless rabble, reveling in their base degeneracy and scorning intellectual enlightenment.

Many a fine spirit who would have served the movement as an effective agitator and powerful advocate, stung to the quick by the keen lash in the hands of a "comrade," has dropped into silence and faded into obscurity.

Fortunately the influence of these self-appointed censors is waning. The movement is no longer a mere fanatical sect. It has outgrown that period in spite of its sentinels and doorkeepers.

Between watchful devotion, which guards against impostors and chronic heresy hunting, which places a premium upon dirt and stupidity, and imposes a penalty upon brains and self-respect, there is a difference wide as the sea. The former is a virtue which cannot be too highly commended, the latter a vice which cannot be too severely condemned.

Thomas McGrady was an absolutely honest man. Almost ten years of intimate and varied relations with him enables the writer to conscientiously pay him this tribute—to place this perennial flower where he sleeps.

No attempt is made to convert our deceased comrade into a saint. Could he speak he would not be shorn of his foibles. Like all great souls he had his faults—the faults that attested his humanity and brought into more perfect relief the many virtues which adorned his manly character and enriched his noble life.

Thomas McGrady found joy in social service and his prefect consecration to his social ideals was the crowning glory of his life and the bow of promise at his death.

Appeal to Reason, December 14, 1907.

Revolution

This is the first and only International Labor Day. It belongs to the working class and is dedicated to the Revolution.

Today the slaves of all the world are taking a fresh breath in the long and weary march; pausing a moment to clear their lungs and shout for joy; celebrating in festal fellowship their coming Freedom.

All hail the Labor Day of May!

The day of the proletarian protest;

The day of stern resolve;

The day of noble aspiration.

Raise high this day the blood-red Standard of the Revolution!

The banner of the Workingmen;

The flag, the only flag, of Freedom.

Slavery, even the most abject—dumb and despairing as it may seem—has yet its inspiration. Crushed it may be, but extinguished never. Chain the slave as you will, O Masters, brutalize him as you may, yet in his soul, though dead, he yearns for freedom still.

The great discovery the modern slaves have made is that they themselves their freedom must achieve. This is the secret of their solidarity; the heart of their hope; the inspiration that nerves them all with sinews of steel.

They are still in bondage, but no longer cower;

No longer grovel in the dust,

But stand erect like men.

Conscious of their growing power the future holds out to them her outstretched hands.

As the slavery of the working class is international, so the movement for its emancipation.

The salutation of slave to slave this day is repeated in every human tongue as it goes ringing round the world.

The many millions are at last awakening. For countless ages they have suffered; drained to the dregs the bitter cup of misery and woe.

At last, at last the historic limitation has been reached, and soon a new sun will light the world.

Red is the life-tide of our common humanity and red our symbol of universal kinship. Tyrants deny it; fear it; tremble with rage and terror when they behold it.

We reaffirm it and on this day pledge anew our fidelity—come life or death—to the blood-red Banner of the Revolution.

Socialist greetings this day to all our fellow-workers! To the god-like souls in Russia marching grimly, sublimely into the jaws of hell with the Song of the Revolution in their death-rattle; to the Orient, the Occident and all the Isles of the Sea!

VIVE LA REVOLUTION!

The most heroic word in all languages is REVOLUTION. It thrills and vibrates; cheers and inspires. Tyrants and time-servers fear it, but the oppressed hail it with joy.

The throne trembles when this throbbing word is lisped, but to the hovel it is food for the famishing and hope for the victims of despair.

Let us glorify today the revolutions of the past and hail the Great Revolution yet to come before Emancipation shall make all the days of the year May Days of peace and plenty for the sons and daughters of toil.

It was with Revolution as his theme that Mark Twain's soul drank deep from the fount of inspiration. His immortality will rest at last upon this royal tribute to the French Revolution;

"The ever memorable and blessed revolution, which swept a thousand years of villainy away in one swift tidal wave of blood—one: a settlement of that hoary debt in the proportion of half a drop of blood for each hogshead of it that had been pressed by slow tortures out of that people in the weary stretch of ten centuries of wrong and shame and misery the like of which was not to be mated but in hell. There were two Reigns of Terror, if we would but remember it and consider it: the one wrought murder in hot passion, the other in heartless cold blood; the one lasted mere months, the other lasted a thousand years; the one inflicted death on ten thousand persons, the other upon a hundred millions; but our shudders are all for the horrors of the minor Terror, so to speak; whereas, what is the horror of swift death by the axe compared with lifelong death from hunger, cold, insult, cruelty and heartbreak? What is swift death by lightning compared with death by slow fire at the stake? A city cemetery could contain the coffins filled by that brief Terror, which we have all been so diligently taught to shiver at and mourn over, but all France could hardly contain the coffins filled by that older and real Terror which none of us has been taught to see in its vastness or pity as it deserves."

New York Worker, April 27, 1907.

Letter from Debs on immigration

My Dear Brewer:—

Have just read the majority report of the Committee on Immigration. It is utterly unsocialistic, reactionary and in truth outrageous, and I hope you will oppose [it] with all your power. The plea that certain races are to be excluded because of tactical expediency would be entirely consistent in a bourgeois convention of self-seekers, but should have no place in a proletarian gathering under the auspices of an international movement that is calling on the oppressed and exploited workers of all the world to unite for their emancipation...

Away with the "tactics" which require the exclusion of the oppressed and suffering slaves who seek these shores with the hope of bettering their wretched condition and are driven back under the cruel lash of expediency by those who call themselves Socialists in the name of a movement whose proud boast it is that it stands uncompromisingly for the oppressed and down-trodden of all the earth. These poor slaves have just as good a right to enter here as even the authors of this report who now seek to exclude them. The only difference is that the latter had the advantage of a little education and had not been so cruelly ground and oppressed, but in point of principle there is no difference, the motive of all being precisely the same, and if the convention which meets in the name of Socialism should discriminate at all it should be in favor of the miserable races who have borne the heaviest burdens and are most nearly crushed to the earth.

Upon this vital proposition I would take my stand against the world and no specious argument of subtle and sophistical defenders of the Civic Federation unionism, who do not hesitate to sacrifice principle for numbers and jeopardize ultimate success for immediate gain, could move me to turn my back upon the oppressed, brutalized and despairing victims of the old world, who are lured to these shores by some faint glimmer of hope that here their crushing burdens may be lightened, and some star of promise rise in their darkened skies.

The alleged advantages that would come to the Socialist movement because of such heartless exclusion would all be swept away a thousand times by the sacrifice of a cardinal principle of the international Socialist movement, for well might the good faith of such a movement be questioned by intelligent workers if it placed itself upon record as barring its doors against the very races most in need of relief, and extinguishing their hope, and leaving them in dark despair at the very time their ears were first attuned to the international call and their hearts were beginning to throb responsive to the solidarity of the oppressed of all lands and all climes beneath the skies.

In this attitude there is nothing of maudlin sentimentality, but simply a rigid adherence to fundamental principles of the international proletarian movement. If Socialism, international revolutionary Socialism, does not stand staunchly, unflinchingly, and uncompromisingly for the working class and for the exploited and oppressed masses of all lands, then it stands for none and its claim is a false pretense and its profession a delusion and a snare.

Let those desert us who will because we refuse to shut the international door in the faces of their own brethren; we will be none the weaker but all the stronger for their going, for they evidently have no clear conception of the international solidarity, are wholly lacking in the revolutionary spirit, and have no proper place in the Socialist movement while they entertain such aristocratic notions of their own assumed superiority.

Let us stand squarely on our revolutionary, working class principles and make our fight openly and uncompromisingly against all our enemies, adopting no cowardly tactics and holding out no false hopes, and our movement will then inspire the faith, arouse the spirit, and develop the fibre that will prevail against the world.

Yours without compromise,
EUGENE V. DEBS

International Socialist Review, January, 1910.
International Socialist Review, July, 1910.

Working class politics

We live in the capitalist system, so-called because it is dominated by the capitalist class. In this system the capitalists are the rulers and the workers the subjects. The capitalists are in a decided minority and yet they rule because of the ignorance of the working class.

So long as the workers are divided, economically and politically, they will remain in subjection, exploited of what they produce and treated with contempt by the parasites who live out of their labor.

The economic unity of the workers must first be effected before there can be any progress toward emancipation. The interests of the millions of wage workers are identical, regardless of nationality, creed or sex, and if they will only open their eyes to this simple, self-evident fact, the greatest obstacle will have been overcome and the day of victory will draw near.

The primary need of the workers is industrial unity and by this I mean their organization in the industries in which they are employed as a whole instead of being separated into more or less impotent unions according to their crafts. Industrial unionism is the only effective means of economic organization and the quicker the workers realize this and unite within one compact body for the good of all, the sooner will they cease to be the victims of ward-heeling labor politicians and accomplish something of actual benefit to themselves and those dependent upon them. In Chicago where the labor grafters, posing as union leaders, have so long been permitted to thrive in their iniquity, there is especially urgent need of industrial unionism, and when this is fairly under way it will express itself politically in a class conscious vote of and for the working class.

So long as the workers are content with conditions as they are, so long as they are satisfied to belong to a craft union under the leadership of those who are far more interested in drawing their own salaries and feathering their own nests with graft than in the welfare of their followers, so long, in a word, as the workers are meek and submissive followers, mere sheep, they will be fleeced, and no one will hold them in greater contempt than the very grafters and parasites who fatten out of their misery.

It is not Gompers, who banquets with Belmont and Carnegie,

---

and Mitchell, who is paid and pampered by the plutocrats, who are going to unite the workers in their struggle for emancipation. The Civic Federation, which was organized by the master class and consists of plutocrats, politicians and priests, in connivance with so-called labor leaders, who are used as decoys to give that body the outward appearance of representing both capital and labor, is the staunch supporter of trade-unions and the implacable foe of industrial unionism and Socialism, and this in itself should be sufficient to convince every intelligent worker that the trade union under its present leadership and, as now used, is more beneficial to the capitalist class than it is to the workers, seeing that it is the means of keeping them disunited and pitted against each other, and as an inevitable result, in wage slavery.

The workers themselves must take the initiative in uniting their forces for effective economic and political action; the leaders will never do it for them. They must no longer suffer themselves to be deceived by the specious arguments of their betrayers, who blatantly boast of their unionism that they may traffic in it and sell out the dupes who blindly follow them. I have very little use for labor leaders in general and none at all for the kind who feel their self-importance and are so impressed by their own wisdom that where they lead their dupes are expected to blindly follow without a question. Such "leaders" lead their victims to the shambles and deliver them over for a consideration and this is possible only among craft-divided wage-slaves who are kept apart for the very purpose that they may feel their economic helplessness and rely upon some "leader" to do something for them.

Economic unity will be speedily followed by political unity. The workers once united in one great industrial union will vote a united working class ticket. Not only this, but only when they are so united can they fit themselves to take control of industry when the change comes from wage-slavery to economic freedom. It is precisely because it is the mission of industrial unionism to unite the workers in harmonious co-operation in the industries in which they are employed, and by their enlightened inter-dependence and self-imposed discipline prepare them for industrial mastery and self-control when the hour strikes, thereby backing up with their economic power the verdict they render at the ballot box, it is precisely because of this fact that every Socialist, every class-conscious worker should be an industrial unionist and strive by all the means at his command to unify the workers in the all-embracing bonds of industrial unionism.

The Socialist Party is the party of the workers, organized to express in political terms their determination to break their fetters and rise to the dignity of free men. In this party the workers must unite and develop their political power to conquer and abolish the capitalist political state and clear the way for industrial and social democracy.

But the new order can never be established by mere votes alone. This must be the result of industrial development and intelligent economic and political organization, necessitating both the industrial union and the political party of the workers to achieve their emancipation.

In this work, to be successfully accomplished, woman must have an equal part with man. If the revolutionary movement of the workers stands for anything it stands for the absolute equality of the sexes and when this fact is fully realized and the working woman takes her place side by side with the working man all along the battlefront the great struggle will soon be crowned with victory.

International Socialist Review, November, 1910.

Danger ahead

The large increase in the Socialist vote in the late national and state elections is quite naturally hailed with elation and rejoicing by party member, but I feel prompted to remark in the light of some personal observations during the campaign, that it is not entirely a matter for jubilation. I am not given to pessimism, or captious criticism, and yet I cannot but feel that some of the votes placed to our credit this year were obtained by methods not consistent with the principles of a revolutionary party, and in the long run will do more harm than good.

I yield to no one in my desire to see the party grow and the vote increase, but in my zeal I do not lose sight of the fact that healthy growth and a substantial vote depend upon efficient organization, the self-education and self-discipline of the membership, and that where these are lacking, an inflated vote secured by compromising methods, can only be hurtful to the movement.

The danger I see ahead is that the Socialist Party at this stage, and under existing conditions, is apt to attract elements which it cannot assimilate, and that it may be either weighted down, or torn asunder with internal strife, or that it may become permeated and corrupted with the spirit of bourgeois reform to an extent that will practically destroy its virility and efficiency as a revolutionary organization.

To my mind the working class character and the revolutionary integrity of the Socialist Party are of first importance. All the votes of the people would do us no good if our party ceased to be a revolutionary party, or only incidentally so, while yielding more and more to the pressure to modify the principles and program of the party for the sake of swelling the vote and hastening the day of its expected triumph.

It is precisely this policy and the alluring promise it holds out to new members with more zeal than knowledge of working class economics that constitutes the danger we should guard against in preparing for the next campaign. The truth is that we have not a few members who regard vote-getting as of supreme importance, no matter by what method the votes may be secured, and this leads them to hold out inducements and make representations which are not at all compatible with the stern and uncompromising principles of a revolutionary party. They seek to make the Socialist propaganda so attractive—eliminating whatever may give offense to bourgeois sensibilities—that it serves as a bait for votes rather than as a means of education, and votes thus secured do not properly belong to us and do injustice to our party as well as to those who cast them.

These votes do not express Socialism and in the next ensuing election are quite as apt to be turned against us, and it is better that they be not cast for the Socialist Party, registering a degree of progress the party is not entitled to and indicating a political position the party is unable to sustain.

Socialism is a matter of growth, of evolution, which can be advanced by wise methods, but never by obtaining for it a fictitious vote. We should seek only to register the actual vote of Socialism, no more and no less. In our propaganda we should state our principles clearly, speak the truth fearlessly, seeking neither to flatter nor to offend, but only to convince those who should be with us and win them to our cause through an intelligent understanding of its mission.

There is also a disposition on the part of some to join hands with reactionary trade-unionists in local emergencies and in certain temporary situations to effect some specific purpose, which may or may not be in harmony with our revolutionary program. No possible good can come from any kind of a political alliance, expressed or implied, with trade-unions or the leaders of trade unions who are opposed to Socialism and only turn to it for use in some extremity, the fruit of their own reactionary policy.

Of course we want the support of trade-unionists, but only of those who believe in Socialism and are ready to vote and work with us for the overthrow of capitalism.

The American Federation of Labor, as an organization, with its Civic Federation to determine its attitude and control its course, is deadly hostile to the Socialist Party and to any and every revolutionary movement of the working class. To kow-tow to this organization and to join hands with its leaders to secure political favors can only result in compromising our principles and bringing disaster to the party.

Not for all the vote of the American Federation of Labor and its labor-dividing and corruption-breeding craft-unions should we compromise one jot of our revolutionary principles; and if we do we shall be visited with the contempt we deserve by all real Socialists, who will scorn to remain in a party professing to be a revolutionary party of the working class while employing the crooked and disreputable methods of ward-heeling and politicians to attain their ends.

Of far greater importance than increasing the vote of the Socialist Party is the economic organization of the working class. To the extent, and only to the extent, that the workers are organized and disciplined in their respective industries can the Socialist movement advance and the Socialist Party hold what is registered by the ballot. The election of legislative and administrative officers, here and there, where the party is still in a crude state and the members economically unprepared and politically unfit to assume the responsibilities thrust upon them as the result of popular discontent, will inevitably bring trouble and set the party back, instead of advancing it, and while this is to be expected and is to an extent unavoidable, we should court no more of that kind of experience than is necessary to avoid a repetition of it. The Socialist Party has already achieved some victories of this kind which proved to be defeats, crushing and humiliating, and from which the party has not even now, after many years, entirely recovered.

We have just so much Socialism that is stable and dependable, because securely grounded in economics, in discipline, and all else that expresses class-conscious solidarity, and this must be augmented steadily through economic and political organization, but no amount of mere votes can accomplish this in even the slightest degree.

Voting for Socialism is not Socialism any more than a menu is a meal.

Socialism must be organized, drilled, equipped and the place to begin is in the industries where the workers are employed. Their economic power has got to be developed through sufficient organization, or their political power, even if it could be developed, would but react upon them, thwart their plans, blast their hopes, and all but destroy them.

Such organization to be effective must be expressed in terms of industrial unionism. Each industry must be organized in its entirety, embracing all the workers, and all working together in the interest of all, in the true spirit of solidarity, thus laying the foundation and developing the superstructure of the new system within the old, from which it is evolving, and systematically fitting the workers, step by step, to assume entire control of the productive forces when the hour strikes for the impending organic change.

Without such economic organization and the economic power with which it is clothed, and without the industrial co-operative training, discipline and efficiency which are its corollaries, the fruit of any political victories the workers may achieve will turn to ashes on their lips.

Now that the capitalist system is so palpably breaking down, and in consequence its political parties breaking up, the disintegrating elements with vague reform ideas and radical bourgeois tendencies will head in increasing numbers toward the Socialist Party, especially since the greatly enlarged vote of this year has been announced and the party is looming up as a possible means, and in fact, the only effectual means of securing the party against such a fatality is the economic power of the industrially-organized workers.

The votes will come rapidly enough from now on without seeking them and we should make it clear that the Socialist Party wants the votes only of those who want Socialism, and that, above all, as a revolutionary party of the working class, it discountenances vote-seeking for the sake of votes and holds in contempt office-seeking for the sake of office. These belong entirely to capitalist parties with their bosses and their boodle and have no place in a party whose shibboleth is emancipation.

With the workers efficiently organized industrially, bound together by the common tie of their enlightened self-interest, they will just as naturally and inevitably express their economic solidarity in political terms and cast a united vote for the party of their class as the forces of nature express obedience to the laws of gravitation.

International Socialist Review, January, 1911.

Danger ahead

The crisis in Mexico

Now that Diaz is overthrown and his administration is a thing of the past, what of the Mexican revolution and the future? Will the substitution of Madero or some other landed aristocrat and bourgeois political reformer placate the people and end the revolution? Let us hope not, and yet it takes but very little in the way of concession to satisfy the ignorant and oppressed masses.

The mere overthrow of Diaz of itself means little to the Mexican people. Their condition will remain substantially the same under the new regime, and yet this change of administration with its attendant circumstances marks an epoch in the history of the Mexican nation. Certain political reforms will be instituted as concessions to the people and while economic conditions will remain substantially as they have been the people have been inspirited by the revolutionary movement and the concessions made to them will but stimulate their ardor in the struggle to overthrow not merely their political dictators but their economic exploiters, and they will never cease their agitation until they have achieved their emancipation.

The real crisis in Mexico, as it seems to me, is now at hand. What the results of the approaching election may be or what the successor of Diaz may or may not do in the way of political reform are of little consequence compared to what the revolutionists will do in this crisis. Will they be able to keep their forces intact and unite in carrying on the fight along lines leading most directly to their emancipation? Most earnestly do I hope so and yet it is almost too much to expect. Already there are signs of dissension among the revolutionists themselves which threaten grave results to their movement.

As one who realizes in some measure the gravity of the situation our comrades are facing in Mexico and the vital concern of the entire working class of America in that situation, and as one whose whole heart has been with the Mexican revolutionary movement since its inception, I feel moved to declare what I believe to be the only safe course for our Mexican comrades to pursue to reach the end they have in view. It is with no desire to obtrude myself and in no spirit of dictation that I now speak, but solely from a desire to do my duty toward our Mexican comrades as I understand that duty.

First of all, the masses of Mexican workers and producers, like those of other countries, are ignorant, superstitious, unorganized and all but helpless in their slavish subjugation. In their present demoralized state economic emancipation is simply out of the question. They must first be reached and aroused, educated and organized, and until this work is accomplished to at least some extent all hope of successful revolution is doomed to disappointment.

It is well enough for the leaders of the Mexican Liberal Party to declare that this is an "economic revolution," but do the masses so understand it, and are they consciously aiming at such an end? And until they are in some degree class conscious and fitted by training and discipline for economic mastery, is not the success of such a revolution utterly out of the question?

If I read aright the manifesto recently issued by the Mexican Liberal Party all political action is tabooed. "Direct action," so-called, is relied upon for results. Reading between the lines I can see nothing but anarchism in this program and if that is what the leaders mean they should frankly say so that there may be no misunderstanding as to their attitude and program. Of course they have the right to take any position they may think proper, the same right that I have to disagree with them, and frankly, if I correctly understand their position it is not calculated to promote but rather to put off the revolutionary end they have in view.

The anarchistic attitude the leaders seem to have assumed and the "direct action" they contemplate, if persisted in, will eventuate, in my opinion, in a series of Haymarket sacrifices and the useless shedding of their noblest blood.

The battle-cry of the Mexican Liberal Party is, "Land and Liberty," and its leaders declare that "the taking away of the land from the hands of the rich must be accomplished during the present insurrection." If the land can be taken from the rich in this insurrection so can also the mills, factories, mines, railroads, and the machinery of production, and the question is, what would the masses in their present ignorant and unorganized state do with them after having obtained them? It would simply add calamity to their calamities, granting that this impossible feat were capable of achievement.

It seems to me that the leaders of the Mexican Liberal Party, whose honesty is unquestioned and whose ability and attainments are of a high order, underestimate the magnitude and malignity of the power they are dealing with. They propose to take the lands from the rich, dispossess them at one swoop, when they are scarcely organized, while the rich control all the armies and navies of the world. The present insurrection has accomplished much but it can not be expected to accomplish everything, least of all economic revolution over night.

When the leaders of the Mexican Liberal Party undertake to transfer the lands from the rich to the poor, that hour they attack the armed forces of capitalism, which means the United States as well as Mexico. The lands in Mexico belong in large part to American capitalists and they will fight for them to the last ditch and with all the powerful resources at their command.

Let not the Mexican revolutionists depend too much on the "International Committee of the Mexican Liberal Party Junta" which they propose organizing "in all the principal cities of the United States and Europe." That some effective co-operation may thus be secured is entirely probable, but our Mexican comrades who saw their own leaders thrown into American prisons with scarcely a protest except among the Socialists are apt to be disappointed if they rely to any great extent upon the enslaved working classes of other countries whose energies are all absorbed in their own struggle for existence.

The right course for the Mexican revolutionists to pursue in this crisis, in my opinion, is to lay the foundation for economic and political organization of the dispossessed and enslaved masses, throughout the republic. This may seem to be too painfully slow in such an extreme exigency, but it will prove in the end to be not only the most direct road but the only road out of the wilderness.

The historic process must be taken into account by our Mexican comrades. There is no short cut to economic freedom. Power is necessary to achieve it, the power that springs from right education and organization, and this power in the present struggle is both economic and political, and to refuse to develop and exercise either is folly that is certain to end in disaster.

When the Mexican revolutionary leaders renounce all political action as unclean and demoralizing and when they express their abhorrence of all class-conscious political activity as simply vicious illusion "dreamed of in the opium den of politics," they align themselves with the anarchists and virtually repudiate and renounce the international Socialist movement.

If this is not their attitude I must confess I do not understand it; if it is their attitude, their dream of establishing anarchist-communism

---

in Mexico at this stage of its industrial and social development will be rudely dispelled before many days.

The workers of all other countries are turning to the international Socialist movement and developing their economic and political power to carry out its program of emancipation and that is what they will have to do in Mexico. Other countries have had their insurrections and revolutions, their dreams and hopes of sudden emancipation, but they have all had to settle down at last to the education and organization of the masses as the only possible means of attaining that end.

The overthrow of Diaz will mean at least, I take it, the right to organize the working class and this is the work that should be taken in hand with all the energy that can be brought to bear upon it.

Here is virgin soil for industrial unionism and all the workers should be organized as speedily as possible within one great industrial organization and at the same time united politically within the Socialist Party. This is the most direct action I know and I have had experience enough to be satisfied at least in my own mind that what is now so urgently advocated by some as direct action is the most indirect and fruitless action that could possibly be taken.

If the leaders of the Mexican revolution will in this crisis align themselves with the international working class movement, accept its principles, adopt its program, and then proceed with all their energy to educate and organize, economically and politically, the masses of Mexican peons and wage slaves they will mark the most important era in Mexican history and blaze the way direct to emancipation.

International Socialist Review, July, 1911.

Sound socialist tactics

Socialists are practically all agreed as to the fundamental principles of their movement. But as to tactics there is wide variance among them. The matter of sound tactics, equally with the matter of sound principles, is of supreme importance. The disagreements and dissensions among socialists relate almost wholly to tactics. The party splits which have occurred in the past have been due to same cause, and if the party should ever divide again, which it is to be hoped it will not, it will be on the rock of tactics.

Revolutionary tactics must harmonize with revolutionary principles. We could better hope to success with reactionary principles and revolutionary tactics than with revolutionary principles and reactionary tactics.

The matter of tactical differences should be approached with open mind and in the spirit of tolerance. The freest discussion should be allowed. We have every element in every shade of capitalist society in our party, and we are in for a lively time at the very best before we work out these differences and settle down to a policy of united and constructive work for Socialism instead of spending so much time and energy lampooning one another.

In the matter of tactics we cannot be guided by the precedents of other countries. We have to develop our own and they must be adapted to the American people and to American conditions. I am not sure that I have the right idea about tactics; I am sure only that I appreciate their importance, that I am open to correction, and that I am ready to change whenever I find myself wrong.

It seems to me there is too much rancor and too little toleration among us in the discussion of our differences. Too often the spirit of criticism is acrid and hypercritical. Personal animosities are engendered, but opinions remain unchanged. Let us waste as little as possible of our militant spirit upon one another. We shall need it all for our capitalist friends.

There has recently been some rather spirited discussion about a paragraph which appears in the pamphlet on "Industrial Socialism," by William D. Haywood and Frank Bohn. The paragraph follows:

"When the worker, either through experience or study of Socialism, comes to know this truth, he acts accordingly. *He retains abso-*

lutely no respect for the property 'rights' of the profit-takers. He will use any weapon which will win his fight. He knows that the present laws of property are made by and for the capitalists. *Therefore he does not hesitate to break them."*

The sentences which I have italicized provoked the controversy.

We have here a matter of tactics upon which a number of comrades of ability and prominence have sharply disagreed. For my own part I believe the paragraph to be entirely sound.

Certainly all Socialists, knowing how and to what end capitalist property "rights" are established, must hold such "rights" in contempt. In the *Manifesto* Marx says: "The Communist (Socialist) revolution is the most radical rupture with traditional property relations; no wonder that its development involves the most radical rupture with traditional ideas."

As a revolutionist I can have no respect for capitalist property laws, nor the least scruple about violating them. I hold all such laws to have been enacted through chicanery, fraud and corruption, with the sole end in view of dispossessing, robbing and enslaving the working class. But this does not imply that I propose making an individual law-breaker of myself and butting my head against the stone wall of existing property laws. That might be called force, but it would not be that. It would be mere weakness and folly.

If I had the force to overthrow these despotic laws I would use it without an instant's hesitation or delay, but I haven't got it, and so I am law-abiding under protest—not from scruple—and bide my time.

Here let me say that for the same reason I am opposed to sabotage and to "direct action." I have not a bit of use for the "propaganda of the deed." These are the tactics of anarchist individualists and not of Socialist collectivists. They were developed by and belong exclusively to our anarchist friends and accord perfectly with their philosophy. These and similar measures are reactionary, not revolutionary, and they invariably have a demoralizing effect upon the following of those who practice them. If I believed in the doctrine of violence and destruction as party policy; if I regarded the class struggle as guerrilla warfare, I would join the anarchists and practice as well as preach such tactics.

It is not because these tactics involve the use of force that I am opposed to them, but because they do not. The physical forcist is the victim of his own boomerang. The blow he strikes reacts upon himself and his followers. The force that implies power is utterly lacking, and it can never be developed by such tactics.

The foolish and misguided, zealots and fanatics, are quick to applaud and eager to employ such tactics, and the result is usually hurtful to themselves and to the cause they seek to advance.

There have been times in the past, and there are countries today where the frenzied deed of a glorious fanatic like old John Brown seems to have been inspired by Jehovah himself, but I am now dealing with the twentieth century and with the United States.

There may be, too, acute situations arising and grave emergencies occurring, with perhaps life at stake, when recourse to violence might be justified, but a great body of organized workers, such as the Socialist movement, cannot predicate its tactical procedure upon such exceptional instances.

But my chief objection to all these measures is that they do violence to the class psychology of the workers and cannot be successfully inculcated as mass doctrine. The very nature of these tactics adapts them to guerrilla warfare, to the bomb planter, the midnight assassin; and such warfare, in this country, at least, plays directly into the hands of the enemy.

Such tactics appeal to stealth and suspicion, and cannot make for solidarity. The very teaching of sneaking and surreptitious practices has a demoralizing effect and a tendency to place those who engage in them in the category of "Black Hand" agents, dynamiters, safe-blowers, hold-up men, burglars, thieves and pickpockets.

If sabotage and direct action, as I interpret them, were incorporated in the tactics of the Socialist Party, it would at once be the signal for all the *agents provocateurs* and police spies in the country to join the party and get busy. Every solitary one of them would be a rabid "direct actionist," and every one would safely make his "get-away" and secure his reward, a la McPartland, when anything was "pulled off" by their dupes, leaving them with their necks in the nooses.

With the sanctioning of sabotage and similar practices the Socialist Party would stand responsible for the deed of every spy or madman, the seeds of strife would be subtly sown in the ranks, mutual suspicion would be aroused, and the party would soon be torn into warring factions to the despair of the betrayed workers and the delight of their triumphant masters.

If sabotage or any other artifice of direct action could be successfully employed, it would be wholly unnecessary, as better results could be accomplished without it. To the extent that the working class has power based upon class-consciousness, force is unnecessary; to the extent that power is lacking, force can only result in harm.

I am opposed to any tactics which involve stealth, secrecy, intrigue, and necessitate acts of individual violence for their execution.

The work of the Socialist movement must all be done out in the broad open light of day. Nothing can be done by stealth that can be of any advantage to it in this country.

The workers can be emancipated only by their own collective will, the power inherent in themselves as a class, and this collective will and conquering power can only be the result of education, enlightenment and self-imposed discipline.

Sound tactics are constructive, not destructive. The collective reason of the workers repels the idea of individual violence where they are free to assert themselves by lawful and peaceable means.

The American workers are law-abiding and no amount of sneering or derision will alter that fact. Direct action will never appeal to any considerable number of them while they have the ballot and the right of industrial and political organization.

Its tactics alone have prevented the growth of the Industrial Workers of the World. Its principles of industrial unionism are sound, but its tactics are not. Sabotage repels the American worker. He is ready for the industrial union, but he is opposed to the "propaganda of the deed," and as long as the I. W. W. adheres to its present tactics and ignores political action, or treats it with contempt by advising the workers to "strike at the ballot box with an ax," they will regard it as an anarchist organization, and it will never be more than a small fraction of the labor movement.

The sound education of the workers and their thorough organization, both economic and political, on the basis of the class struggle, must precede their emancipation. Without such education and organization they can make no substantial progress, and they will be robbed of the fruits of any temporary victory they may achieve, as they have been through all the centuries of the past.

For one, I hope to see the Socialist Party place itself squarely on record at the coming national convention against sabotage and every other form of violence and destructiveness suggested by what is known as "direct action."

Sound socialist tactics

It occurs to me that the Socialist Party ought to have a standing committee on tactics. The art or science of proletarian party tactics might well enlist the serious consideration of our clearest thinkers and most practical propagandists.

To return for a moment to the paragraph above quoted from the pamphlet of Haywood and Bohn. I agree with them that in their fight against capitalism the workers have a right to use any weapon that will help them to win. It should not be necessary to say that this does not mean the black-jack, the dirk, the lead-pipe or the sawed-off shot-gun. The use of these weapons does not help the workers to win, but to lose, and it would be ridiculous to assume that they were in the minds of the authors when they penned that paragraph.

The sentence as it reads is sound. It speaks for itself and requires no apology. The workers will use any weapon which will help them *win* their fight.

The most powerful and the all-sufficient weapons are the industrial union and the Socialist Party, and they are not going to commit suicide by discarding these and resorting to the sling-shot, the dagger and the dynamite bomb.

Another matter of party concern is the treatment of so-called "intellectuals" in the Socialist movement. Why the term "intellectual" should be one of reproach in the Socialist Party is hard to understand, and yet there are many Socialists who sneer at a man of intellect as if he were an interloper and out of place among Socialists. For myself I am always glad to see a man of brains, of intellect, join the movement. If he comes to us in good faith he is a distinct acquisition and is entitled to all the consideration due to any other comrade.

To punish a man for having brains is rather an anomalous attitude for an educational movement. The Socialist Party, above every other, should offer a premium on brains, intellectual capacity, and attract to itself all the mental forces that can be employed to build up the Socialist movement, that it may fulfill its emancipating mission.

Of course the Socialist movement is essentially a working class movement, and I believe that as a rule party officials and representatives, and candidates for public office, should be chosen from the ranks of the workers. The intellectuals in office should be the exceptions, as they are in the rank and file.

There is sufficient ability among the workers for all official demands, and if there is not, it should be developed without further delay. It is their party, and why should it not be officered and represented by themselves?

An organization of intellectuals would not be officered and represented by wage-earners; neither should an organization of wage-earners be officered by intellectuals.

There is plenty of useful work for the intellectuals to do without holding office, and the more intellectual they are the greater can their service be to the movement. Lecturers, debaters, authors, writers, artists, cartoonists, statisticians, etc., are in demand without number, and the intellectuals can serve to far better advantage in those capacities than in official position.

I believe, too, in rotation in office. I confess to a prejudice against officialism and a dread of bureaucracy. I am a thorough believer in the rank and file, and in *ruling* from the *bottom up* instead of *being ruled* from the *top down*. The natural tendency of officials is to become bosses. They come to imagine that they are indispensable and unconsciously shape their acts to keep themselves in office.

The officials of the Socialist Party should be its servants, and all temptation to yield to the baleful influence of officialism should be removed by constitutional limitation of tenure.

There is a tendency in some states to keep the list of locals a solemn secret. The sheep have got to be protected against the wolves. No one must know what locals there are, or who its officials, for fear they may be corrupted by outside influences. This is an effective method for herding sheep, but not a good way to raise men. If the locals must be guarded against the wolves on the outside, then some one is required to guard them, and that some one is a boss, and it is the nature of the boss to be jealous of outside influences.

If our locals and the members who compose them need the protection of secrecy, they are lacking in the essential revolutionary fiber which can be developed only in the play of the elements surrounding them, and with all the avenues of education and information, and even of miseducation and misinformation, wide open for their reception. They have got to learn to distinguish between their friends and their enemies and between what is wise and what is otherwise and until the rank and file are so educated and enlightened their weakness will sooner or later deliver them as the prey of their enemies.

Still another matter about which there has been not a little ill-natured discussion is the proposed investigation of the Kerr publishing house. I cannot help wondering what business the national committee has making such an investigation. It would be quite as proper, in my opinion, to order an investigation of a building and loan association in which members have their savings invested.

It is true, without a doubt, that the INTERNATIONAL SOCIALIST REVIEW has published articles with which many of us disagreed, but why should it be investigated on that account? Are we Socialists who are constantly protesting against the suppression of free speech now going to set an example of what we propose doing by putting a gag on the lips of our own publications?

I don't agree with a good deal that appears in the REVIEW, and I like it all the better on that account. That is the reason, in fact, why I subscribe for it and read it, and I cannot for the life of me understand why any one would want to suppress it on that account.

If the REVIEW and the concern which publishes it belonged to the national party it would be different, but it does not belong to the party, and the party is in no way responsible for it, and if I were a stockholder I should regard the action of the national committee as the sheerest impertinence and treat it accordingly.

I do not know if the house of Kerr & Co. needs investigating or not. I am satisfied that it does not, but it is none of my business.

The Kerr company consists, as I understand it, of some fifteen hundred stockholders, nearly all of whom are Socialists and none of whom, as far as I am advised, are feeble-minded and in need of a guardian. They have paid in all the money, they own all the stock and they are responsible for the concern; and if they want their publishing business investigated that is their affair and not the affair of the national committee of the Socialist Party.

If the object aimed at is to punish Kerr & Co. and cripple the REVIEW for its advocacy of industrial unionism and for opposing pure and simple craftism, and for keeping open columns and exercising the right of free speech, then it will be found in due time that the uncalled-for investigation of the national committee and the uncomradely spirit which prompted it will have produced the opposite effect.

I cannot close without appealing for both the industrial and political solidarity of the workers.

I thoroughly believe in economic as well as political organization, in the industrial union and in the Socialist Party.

I am an industrial unionist because I am a Socialist and a Socialist because I am an industrial unionist.

I believe in making every effort within our power to promote industrial unionism among the workers and to have them all united in one economic organization. To accomplish this I would encourage industrial independent organization, especially among the millions who have not yet been organized at all, and I would also encourage the "boring from within" for all that can be accomplished by the industrial unionists in the craft unions.

I would have the Socialist Party recognize the historic necessity and inevitability of industrial unionism, and the industrial union reciprocally recognize the Socialist Party, and so declare in the respective preambles to their constitutions.

The Socialist Party cannot be neutral on the union question. It is compelled to declare itself by the logic of evolution, and as a revolutionary party it cannot commit itself to the principles of reactionary unionism. Not only must the Socialist Party declare itself in favor of economic unionism, but the kind of unionism which alone can complement the revolutionary action of the workers on the political field.

I am opposed under all circumstances to any party alliances or affiliations with reactionary trade unions and to compromising tactics of every kind and form, excepting alone in event of some extreme emergency. While the "game of politics," as it is understood and as it is played under capitalist rules, is as repugnant to me as it can possibly be to any one, I am a thorough believer in political organization and political action.

Political power is essential to the workers in their struggle, and they can never emancipate themselves without developing and exercising that power in the interests of their class.

It is not merely in a perfunctory way that I advocate political action, but as one who has faith in proletarian political power and in the efficacy of political propaganda as an educational force in the Socialist movement. I believe in a constructive political program and in electing all the class-conscious workers we can, especially as mayors, judges, sheriffs and as members of the state legislatures and the national Congress.

Sound socialist tactics

The party is now growing rapidly, and we are meeting with some of the trials which are in store for us and which will no doubt subject us to the severest tests. We need to have these trials, which are simply the fires in which we have to be tempered for the work before us.

There will be all kinds of extremists to deal with, but we have nothing to fear from them. Let them all have their day. The great body of the comrades, the rank and file, will not be misled by false teachings or deflected from the true course.

We must put forth all our efforts to control our swelling ranks by the use of wise tactics and to assimilate the accessions to our membership by means of sound education and party discipline.

The new year has opened auspiciously for us, and we have never been in such splendid condition on the eve of a national campaign.

Let us all buckle on our armor and go forth determined to make this year mark an epoch in the social revolution of the United States.

International Socialist Review, February, 1912.

Speech of acceptance

It is with a full sense of the responsibility it imposes and the service it exacts that I accept the nomination for president tendered to me by the Socialist Party of the United States. Personally I did not wish the nomination. It came to me unsought. It came as summons to service and not as a personal honor.

Every true member of the Socialist Party is at the party's service. The confidence of his comrades is to him a sacred trust and their collective will the party's law.

My chief concern as a presidential candidate is that I shall serve well the party, and the class and the cause the party represents.

SOCIALIST PARTY DIFFERENT.

The Socialist Party is fundamentally different from all other parties. It came in the process of evolution and grows with the growth of the forces which created it. Its spirit is militant and its aim revolutionary. It expresses in political terms the aspiration of the working class to freedom and to a larger and fuller life than they have yet known.

The world's workers have always been and still are the world's slaves. They have borne all the burdens of the race and built all the monuments along the track of civilization; they have produced all the world's wealth and supported all the world's governments. They have conquered all things but their own freedom. They are still the subject class in every nation on earth and the chief function of every government is to keep them at the mercy of their masters.

The workers in the mills and factories, in the mines and on the farms and railways never had a party of their own until the Socialist Party was organized. They divided their votes between the parties of their masters. They did not realize that they were using their ballots to forge their own fetters.

But the awakening came. It was bound to come. Class rule became more and more oppressive and wage slavery more and more galling. The eyes of the workers began to open. They began to see the cause of the misery they had dumbly suffered so many years. It dawned upon them that society was divided into two classes—capitalists and workers, exploiters and producers; that the capitalists, while comparatively few, owned the nation and controlled the government; that the courts and the soldiers were at their command, and that the workers, while in a great majority, were in slavish subjection.

When they ventured to protest they were discharged and found themselves blacklisted; when they went out on strike they were suppressed by the soldiers and sent to jail.

They looked about them and saw a land of wonderful resources; they saw the productive machinery made by their own hands and the vast wealth produced by their own labor, in the shadow of which their wives and children were perishing in the skeleton clutch of famine.

BEGAN TO THINK.

The very suffering they were forced to endure quickened their sense. They began to think. A new light dawned upon their dark skies. They rubbed the age-long sleep from their eyes. They had long felt the brutalizing effect of class rule; now they saw the cause of it. Slowly but steadily they became class-conscious. They said, "We are brothers, we are comrades," and they saw themselves multiplied by millions. They caught the prophetic battle-cry of Karl Marx, the world's greatest labor leader, the inspired evangel of working-class emancipation, "Workers of all countries, unite!"

Speech of acceptance   121

And now, behold! The international Socialist movement spreads out over all the nations of the earth. The world's workers are aroused at last. They are no longer on their knees; their bowed bodies are now erect. Despair has given way to hope, weakness to strength, fear to courage. They no longer cringe and supplicate; they hold up their heads and command. They have ceased to fear their masters and have learned to trust themselves.

And this is how the Socialist Party came to be born. It was quickened into life in the bitter struggle of the world's enslaved workers. It expresses their collective determination to break their fetters and emancipate themselves and the race.

Is it strange that the workers are loyal to such a party, that they proudly stand beneath its blazing banners and fearlessly proclaim its conquering principles? It is the one party of their class, born of their agony and baptized in the blood of their countless brethren who perished in the struggle to give it birth.

Hail to this great party of the toiling millions whose battle-cry is heard around the world!

DOESN'T PLEAD FOR VOTES.

We do not plead for votes; the workers give them freely the hour they understand.

But we need to destroy the prejudice that still exists and dispel the darkness that still prevails in the working class world. We need the clear light of sound education and the conquering power of economic and political organization.

Before the unified hosts of labor all the despotic governments on earth are powerless and all resistance vain. Before their onward march all ruling classes disappear and all slavery vanishes forever.

The appeal of the Socialist Party is to all the useful people of the nation, all who work with brain and muscle to produce the nation's wealth and who promote its progress and conserve its civilization.

Only they who bear its burdens may rightfully enjoy the blessings of civilized society.

There are no boundary lines to separate race from race, sex from sex or creed from creed in the Socialist Party. The common rights of all are equally recognized.

Every human being is entitled to sunlight and air, to what his labor produces, and to an equal chance with every other human being to unfold and ripen and give to the world the riches of his mind and soul.

Economic slavery is the world's greatest curse today. Poverty and misery, prostitution, insanity and crime are its inevitable results.

The Socialist Party is the one party which stands squarely and uncompromisingly for the abolition of industrial slavery; the one party pledged in every fibre of its being to the economic freedom of all the people.

So long as the nation's resources and productive and distributive machinery are the private property of a privileged class the masses will be at their mercy, poverty will be their lot and life will be shorn of all that raises it above the brute level.

NEW PROGRESSIVE PARTY.

The infallible test of a political party is the private ownership of the sources of wealth and the means of life. Apply that test to the Republican, Democratic and Progressive parties and upon that basic, fundamental issue you will find them essentially one and the same. They differ according to the conflicting interests of the privileged classes, but at bottom they are alike and stand for capitalist class rule and working class slavery.

The new Progressive Party is a party of progressive capitalism. It is lavishly financed and shrewdly advertised. But it stands for the rule of capitalism all the same.

When the owners of the trusts finance a party to put themselves out of business; when they turn over their wealth to the people from whom they stole it and go to work for a living, it will be time enough to consider the merits of the Roosevelt Progressive Party.

One question is sufficient to determine the true status of all these parties. Do they want the workers to own the tools they work with, control their own jobs and secure to themselves the wealth they produce? Certainly not. That is utterly ridiculous and impossible from their point of view.

The Republican, Democratic and Progressive parties all stand for the private ownership by the capitalists of the productive machinery used by the workers, so that the capitalists can continue to filch the wealth produced by the workers.

The Socialist Party is the only party which declares that the tools of labor belong to labor and that the wealth produced by the working class belong to the working class.

Intelligent workingmen are no longer deceived. They know that the struggle in which the world is engaged today is a class struggle

---

Speech of acceptance 123

and that in this struggle the workers can never win by giving their votes to capitalist parties. They have tried this for many years and it has always produced the same result to them.

The class of privilege and pelf has had the world by the throat and the working class beneath its iron-shod hoofs long enough. The magic word of freedom is ringing through the nation and the spirit of intelligent revolt is finding expression in every land beneath the sun.

The solidarity of the working class is the salient force in the social transformation of which we behold the signs upon every hand. Nearer and nearer they are being drawn together in the bonds of unionism; clearer and clearer becomes their collective vision; greater and greater the power that throbs within them.

HOSTS OF FREEDOM.

They are the twentieth-century hosts of freedom who are to destroy all despotisms, topple over all thrones, seize all sceptres of authority and hold them in their own strong hands, tear up all privilege by the roots, and consecrate the earth and all its fullness to the joy and service of all humanity.

It is vain to hope for material relief upon the prevailing system of capitalism. All the reforms that are proposed by the three capitalist parties, even if carried out in good faith, would still leave the working class in industrial slavery.

The working class will never be emancipated by the grace of the capitalist class, but only by overthrowing that class.

The power to emancipate itself is inherent in the working class, and this power must be developed through sound education and applied through sound organization.

It is foolish and self-destructive for workingmen to turn to Republican, Democratic and Progressive parties on election day as it would be for them to turn to the Manufacturers' Association and the Citizens' Alliance when they are striking against starvation wages.

The capitalist class is organized economically and politically to keep the working class in subjection and perpetuate its power as a ruling class. They do not support a working class union nor a working class party. They are not so foolish. They wisely look out for themselves.

The capitalist class despise a working class party. Why should the working class give their support to a capitalist class party?

Capitalist misrule under which workingmen suffer slavery and the most galling injustice exists only because it has workingmen's support. Withdraw that support and capitalism is dead.

The capitalists can enslave and rob the workers only by the consent of the workers when they cast their ballots on election day.

Every vote cast for a capitalist party, whatever its name, is a vote for wage-slavery, for poverty and degradation.

Every vote cast for the Socialist Party, the workers' own party, is a vote for emancipation.

We appeal to the workers and to all who sympathize with them to make their power felt in this campaign. Never before has there been so great an opportunity to strike an effective blow for freedom.

CAPITALISM DOOMED.

Capitalism is rushing blindly to its impending doom. All the signs portend the inevitable breakdown of the existing order. Deep-seated discontent has seized upon the masses. They must indeed be deaf who do not hear the mutterings of the approaching storm.

Poverty, high prices, unemployment, child slavery, widespread misery and haggard want in a land bursting with abundance; prostitution and insanity, suicide and crime, these in solemn numbers tell the tragic story of capitalism's saturnalia of blood and tears and shame as its end draws near.

It is to abolish this monstrous system and the misery and crime which flow from it in a direful and threatening stream that the Socialist Party was organized and now makes its appeal to the intelligence and conscience of the people. Social reorganization is the imperative demand of this world-wide revolutionary movement.

The Socialist Party's mission is not only to destroy capitalist despotism but to establish industrial and social democracy. To this end the workers are steadily organizing and fitting themselves for the day when they shall take control of the people's industries and when the right to work shall be as inviolate as the right to breathe the breath of life.

Standing as it does for the emancipation of the working class from wage-slavery, for the equal rights and opportunities of all men and all women, for the abolition of child labor and the conservation of all childhood, for social self-rule and the equal freedom of all, the Socialist Party is the party of progress, the party of the future, and its triumph will signal the birth of a new civilization and the dawn of a happier day for all humanity.

International Socialist Review, October, 1912.

A plea for solidarity

To the foregoing Webster adds the following definition: "An entire union, or consolidation of interests and responsibilities; fellowship."

The future of labor, the destiny of the working class, depends wholly upon its own solidarity.* The extent to which this has been achieved or is lacking, determines the strength or weakness, the success or failure, of the labor movement.

Solidarity, however, is not a matter of sentiment, but of fact, cold and impassive as the granite foundation of a skyscraper. If the basic elements, identity of interest, clarity of vision, honesty of intent, and oneness of purpose, or any of these is lacking, all sentimental pleas for solidarity and all efforts to achieve it will be alike barren of results.

The identity of interest is inherent in the capitalist system and the machine process, but the remaining elements essential to solidarity have to be developed in the struggle necessary to achieve it, and it is this struggle in which our unions and parties have been torn asunder and ourselves divided and pitted against each other in factional warfare so bitter and relentless as to destroy all hope of solidarity if the driving forces of capitalism did not operate to make it ultimately inevitable. This struggle has waxed with increasing bitterness and severity during the years since the I. W. W. came upon the scene to mark the advent of industrial unionism to supplant the failing craft unionism of a past age.

But there is reason to believe, as it appears to me, that, as it is "darkest just before the dawn," so the factional struggle for solidarity waxes fiercest just before its culmination. The storm of factional contention, in which diverse views and doctrines clashed and were subjected to the ordeal of fire, in which all the weapons of the revolution must be forged and tempered, has largely spent itself, and conditions which gave rise to these contentions have so changed, as was pointed out by the editor in the February REVIEW, that unity of the revolutionary forces now seems near at hand.

Industrial unionism is now, theoretically at least, universally conceded. Even Gompers himself now acknowledges himself an industrial unionist. The logic of industrial development has settled that question and the dissension it gave rise to is practically ended.

For the purpose of this writing the proletariat and the working class are synonymous terms. I know of no essential distinction between skilled and unskilled salary and wage-workers. They are all in the same economic class and in their aggregate constitute the proletariat or working class, and the hair-splitting attempts that are made to differentiate them in the class struggle give rise to endless lines of cleavage and are inimical if not fatal to solidarity.

Webster describes a proletaire as a "low person," "belonging to the commonalty; hence, mean, vile, vulgar." This is a sufficiently explicit definition of the proletaire by his bourgeois master which at the same time defines his status in capitalist society, and it applies to the entire working and producing class; hence the *lower class.*

Such distinction between industrial workers as still persists the machine is reducing steadily to narrower circles and will eventually blot out entirely.

It is now about a century since a few of the skilled and more intelligent workers in the United States began to dimly perceive their identity of interest, and to band themselves together for their mutual protection against the further encroachments of their employers and masters. From that time to this there has been continuous agitation among the workers, now open and pronounced and again under cover and in whispers, according to conditions and opportunities, but never has the ferment ceased and never can it cease until the whole mass has been raised to manhood's level by the leaven of solidarity.

The net result of a hundred years of agitation, education and unification, it must be confessed, is hardly calculated to inspire one with an excess of optimism and yet, to the keen observer, there is abundant cause for satisfaction with the past and for confidence in the future.

After a century of unceasing labors to organize the workers, about one in fourteen now belongs to a union. To put it in another way, fourteen out of every fifteen who are eligible to membership are still outside of the labor movement. At the same relative rate of growth it would require several centuries more to organize a majority of the working class in the United States.

But there are sound reasons for believing that a new era of labor unionism is dawning and that in the near future organized labor is to come more rapidly to fruition and expand to proportions and de-

---

velop power which will compensate in full measure for the slow and painful progress of the past and for all its keen disappointments and disastrous failures; and chief of these reasons is the disintegration and impending fall of reactionary craft unionism and the rise and spread of the revolutionary industrial movement.

Never has the trade union of the past given adequate recognition to the vast army of common laborers, and in its narrow and selfish indifference to these unorganized masses it has weakened its own foundations, played into the hands of its enemies, and finally sealed its own doom.

The great mass of common, unskilled labor, steadily augmented by the machine process, is the granite foundation of the working class and of the whole social fabric, and to ignore or slight this proletarian mass, or fail to recognize its essentially fundamental character, is to build without a foundation and rear a house of scantlings instead of a fortress of defense.

That the I. W. W. recognized this fundamental fact and directed its energies to the awakening and stimulation of the unskilled masses which had until then lain dormant, was the secret of its spread and power and likewise of the terror it inspired in the ruling class, and had it continued as it began, a revolutionary industrial union, recognizing the need of political as well as industrial action, instead of being hamstrung by its own leaders and converted, officially at least, into an anti-political machine, it would today be the most formidable labor organization in America, if not the world. But the time has not yet come, seemingly, for the organic change from craft segregation to industrial solidarity. There must be further industrial evolution and still greater economic pressure brought to bear upon the workers in the struggle with their masters, to force them to disregard the dividing lines of their craft unions and make common cause with their fellow-workers.

The inevitable split in the I. W. W. came and a bitter factional fight followed. The promising industrial organization was on the rocks. Industrial unionism, which had begun to spread in all directions, came almost to a halt. Fortunately about this time the mass strikes broke out, first in the steel and next in the textile industries. Thousands of unskilled and unorganized workers struck, and for a time both factions of the I. W. W. grew apace and waged the warfare against the mill bosses with an amazing display of power and resources. The important part taken by the Socialist Party and its press and speakers in raising funds for the strikers, giving publicity to the issues involved, creating a healthy public sentiment, bringing their political power to bear in forcing a congressional investigation and backing up the I. W. W. and the strikers in every possible way, had much to do with the progress made and the success achieved during this period.

The victory at Lawrence, one of the most decisive and far-reaching ever won by organized workers, triumphantly demonstrated the power and invincibility of industrial unity backed by political solidarity. Without the co-operation and support of the Socialist Party the Lawrence victory would have been impossible, as would also that at Schenectady which followed some time later.

For reasons which came to light after the Lawrence strike, this solidarity was undermined to a considerable extent when the Paterson strike came, and still more so when the Akron strike of the rubber workers followed, both resulting disastrously to the strikers. Both of these strikes were fought with marvelous loyalty and endurance and could and should have been won.

Now again followed the inevitable. The ranks of the I. W. W. were depleted as suddenly as they had filled up. What is there now left of it at McKee's Rocks, at Lawrence, at Paterson, at Akron, in the east; or at Goldfield, Spokane, and San Diego in the west?

Of course the experience is not lost and if only the workers are wise enough to profit by its lessons it will be worth all its terrible cost to its thousands of victims.

These important events have been rapidly sketched for the reason that just now I am more interested in the future than in the past. The conditions under which the I. W. W. was organized almost a decade ago and which soon afterward disrupted its forces and gave rise to the bitter factional feud and the threatening complications which followed, have undergone such changes that now, unless all the signs of today are misleading, there is a solid economic foundation for the merging of the hitherto conflicting elements into a great industrial organization.

The essential basis of such organization must, as I believe, be the same as it was when the I. W. W. was first launched, and to which the Detroit faction of that body still adheres. This faction is cornerstoned in the true principle of unionism in reference to political action.

In the past the political party of the workers has been disrupted because of disagreement about the labor union and the labor union has been disrupted because of disagreement about the political party. It is that rock upon which we have been wrecked in the past and must steer clear of in the future.

Like causes produce like results. Opponents of political action split the I. W. W. and they will split any union that is not composed wholly of anti-political actionists or in which they are not in a hopeless minority. I say this in no hostile spirit. They are entitled to their opinion the same as the rest of us.

At bottom all anti-political actionists are to all intents anarchists, and anarchists and Socialists have never yet pulled together and probably never will.

Now the industrial organization that ignores or rejects political action is as certain to fail as is the political party that ignores or rejects industrial action. Upon the mutually recognized unity and cooperation of the industrial and political powers of the working class will both the union and the party have to be built if real solidarity is to be achieved.

To deny the political equation is to fly in the face of past experience and invite a repetition of the disruption and disaster which have already wrecked the organized forces of industrialism.

The anti-political unionist and the anti-union Socialist are alike illogical in their reasoning and unscientific in their economics. The one harbors the illusion that the capitalist state can be destroyed and its police powers, court injunctions and gatling guns, in short its political institutions, put out of business by letting politics alone, and the other that the industries can be taken over and operated by the workers without being industrially organized and that the Socialist republic can be created by a majority of votes and by political action alone.

It is beyond question, I think, that an overwhelming majority of industrial unionists favor independent political action and that an overwhelming majority of Socialists favor industrial unionism. Now it seems quite clear to me that these forces can and should be united and brought together in harmonious and effective economic and political co-operation.

There is no essential difference between the Chicago and Detroit factions of the I.W.W. except that relating to political action and if I am right in believing that a majority of the rank and file of the Chicago faction favor political action, then there is no reason why this majority should not consolidate with the Detroit faction and thus put an end to the division of these forces. This accomplished, a fresh start for industrial unionism would undoubtedly be made, and with competent organizers to go out into the field among the unorganized, the reunited I.W.W. would grow by leaps and bounds.

The rumblings of revolt in the A.F. of L. prove conclusively that the leaven of industrialism is also doing its work in the trade unions. The miners at their recent Indianapolis convention, in their scathing indictment of Gompers and his ossified "executive council," disclosed their true attitude toward the reactionary and impotent old federation. When Duncan MacDonald declared that Gompers and his official inner circle slaughtered every progressive measure and that the federation under their administration was reactionary to the core and boss-ridden and worse than useless, the indictment was confirmed by a roar of applause.

At the same convention Charles Moyer, president of the Western Federation of Miners, charged that if the strike of the copper miners in Michigan was lost the responsibility would rest upon Gompers and his "executive council." Gompers, notwithstanding this grave charge, left the convention without waiting to face Moyer. He had to catch a train. He remained long enough, however, to solemnly warn the delegates that the two-cent assessment asked for by the W. F. of M. to support the copper strikers would break up his powerful federation.

Almost eighteen years ago the W. F. of M. withdrew from the A. F. of L. in disgust because the financial support (?) it gave to the Leadville strikers did not amount to enough to cover the postage required to mail the appeal to the local union. Today, when the W. F. of M. is again fighting for its life, the copper miners are told that a two-cent assessment to keep them and their families from starving would "bust" the Federation.

And this is the mighty American Federation of Labor, boasting a grand army of more than two million organized workers?

What has the A. F. of L., Gompers and his "executive council," done for the desperately struggling miners of Colorado and Michigan? Practically nothing.

Then why should the miners put up their scanty and hard-earned wages to support Gompers and the A.F. of L.?

The boasted power of this Civic Federationized, Militia of Christified body of reactionary craft union apostles of the Brotherhood of Capital and Labor turns to ashes always when the test comes, and a two-cent assessment, according to its national president, would kill it stone dead.

The United Mine Workers and the Western Federation of Miners, becoming more and more revolutionary in the desperate fight they are compelled to wage for their existence, are bound to merge soon into one great industrial organization, and the same forces that are driving them together will also drive them out of Gompers' federation of craft unions. There are other progressive unions in the A. F. of L. that will follow the secession of the miners and augment the forces of revolutionary unionism.

The consolidated miners and the reunited I. W. W. would draw to themselves all the trade unions with industrial tendencies, and thus would the reactionary federation of craft unions be transformed, from both within and without, into a revolutionary industrial organization.

On the political field there is no longer any valid reason why there should be more than one party. I believe that a majority of both the Socialist Party and the Socialist Labor Party would vote for consolidation, and I hope to see the initiative taken by the rank and file of both at an early day. The unification of the political forces would tend to clear the atmosphere and promote the unification of the forces on the industrial field.

This article is already longer than I intended, but before closing, I want to say that in my opinion, Section six of Article two ought to be stricken from the Socialist Party's constitution. I have not changed my opinion in regard to sabotage, but I am opposed to restricting free speech under any pretense whatsoever, and quite as decidedly opposed to our party seeking favor in bourgeois eyes by protesting that it does not countenance violence and is not a criminal organization.

I believe our party attitude toward sabotage is right, and this attitude is reflected in its propaganda and need not be enforced by constitutional penalties of expulsion. If there is anything in sabotage we should know it, and free discussion will bring it out; if there is nothing in it we need not fear it, and even if it is lawless and hurtful, we are not called upon to penalize it any more than we are theft or any other crime.

The conditions of today, the tendency and the outlook are all that the most ardent Socialists and industrialists could desire, and if all who believe in a united party backed by a united union and a united nation backed by a united party, will now put aside the prejudices created by past dissensions, sink all petty differences, strike hands in comradely concord, and get to work in real earnest, we shall soon have the foremost proletarian revolutionary movement in the world.

We need not only a new alignment and a better mutual understanding, but we need above all the real Socialist spirit, which expresses itself in boundless enthusiasm, energetic action, and the courage to dare and do all things in the service of the cause. We need to *be* comrades in all the term implies and to help and cheer and strengthen one another in the daily struggle. If the "love of comrades" is but a barren ideality in the Socialist movement, then there is no place for it in the heart of mankind.

I appeal to all Socialist comrades and all industrial unionists to join in harmonizing the various elements of the revolutionary movement and in establishing the economic and political solidarity of the workers. If this be done a glorious new era will dawn for the working class in the United States.

International Socialist Review, March, 1914.

* "Solidarity—a word we owe to the French Communists and which signifies a community in gain and loss, in honor and dishonor, a being (so to speak) all in the same bottom—is so convenient that it will be in vain to struggle against its reception."

The gunmen and the miners

The time has come for the United Mine Workers and the Western Federation of Miners to levy a special monthly assessment to create a GUNMEN DEFENSE FUND.

This fund should be sufficient to provide each member with the latest high power rifle, the same as used by the corporation gunmen, and 500 rounds of cartridges.

In addition to this every district should purchase and equip and man enough Gatling and machine guns to match the equipment of Rockefeller's private army of assassins.

This suggestion is made advisedly and I hold myself responsible for every word of it.

The corporations have the right to recruit and maintain private armies of thieves, thugs and ex-convicts to murder striking workingmen, sack their homes, insult their wives, and roast their babes, then labor unions not only have the right but it is their solemn duty to arm themselves to resist these lawless attacks and defend their homes and loved ones.

To the miners especially do these words apply, and to them in particular is this message addressed.

Paint Creek, Calumet and Ludlow are of recent occurrence.

You miners have been forced out on strike, and you have been made the victims of every conceivable method of persecution.

You have been robbed, insulted and treated with contempt; you have seen your wives and babes murdered in cold blood before your eyes.

You have been thrown into foul dungeons where you have lain for months for daring to voice your protest against these cruel outrages, and many of you are now cold in death with the gaping bullet wounds in your bodies to bear mute testimony to the efficacy of government by gunmen as set up in the mining camps by the master class during the last few years.

Under government by gunmen you are literally shorn of the last vestige of liberty and you have absolutely no protection under the law. When you go out on strike, your master has his court issue the injunction that strips you of your power to resist his injustice, and then has his private army of gunmen invade your camp, open fire on your habitations and harass you and your families until the strike is broken and you are starved back into the pits on your master's terms. This has happened over and over again in all the mining states of this union.

Now the private army of gunmen which has been used to break your strikes is an absolutely lawless aggregation.

If you miners were to arm a gang of thugs and assassins with machine guns and repeating rifles and order them to march on the palatial residences of the Rockefellers, riddle them with bullets, and murder the inmates in cold blood, not sparing even the babes, if there happened to be any, how long would it be before your officials would be in jail and your unions throttled and put out of business by the law?

The Rockefellers have not one particle more lawful right to maintain a private army to murder you union men than you union men would have to maintain a private army to murder the Rockefellers.

AND YET THE LAW DOES NOT INTERFERE WITH THE ROCKEFELLERS WHEN THEY SET UP GOVERNMENT BY GUNMEN, AND HAVE THEIR PRIVATE ARMY OF MAN-KILLERS SWOOP DOWN ON A MINING CAMP, TURN LOOSE THEIR MACHINE GUNS, KILL WITHOUT MERCY, AND LEAVE DEATH, AGONY AND DESOLATION IN THEIR WAKE, AND THEREFORE IT BECOMES YOUR SOLEMN DUTY TO ARM YOURSELVES IN DEFENSE OF YOUR HOMES AND IN DRIVING OUT THESE INVADING ASSASSINS, AND PUTTING AN END TO GOVERNMENT BY GUNMEN IN THE UNITED STATES.

In a word, the protection the government owes you and fails to provide, you are morally bound to provide for yourselves.

You have the unquestioned right, under the law, to defend your life and to protect the sanctity of your fireside. Failing in either, you are a coward and a craven and undeserving the name of man.

If a thief or thug attacks you or your wife or child and threatens to take your life, you have a lawful right to defend yourself and your loved ones, even to the extent of slaying the assailant. This right is quite as valid and unimpaired—in fact it is even more inviolate—if the attack is made by a dozen or a hundred, instead of only one.

Rockefeller's gunmen are simply murderers at large, and you have the same right to kill them when they attack you that you have to kill the burglar who breaks into your house at midnight or the highwayman who holds you up at the point of his pistol.

The gunmen and the miners 135

Rockefeller's hired assassins have no lawful right that you miners are bound to respect. They are professional man-killers, the lowest and vilest on earth. They hire out to break your strike, shoot up your home and kill you, and you should have no more compunction in killing them than if they were so many mad-dogs or rattlesnakes that menaced your homes and your community.

Recollect that in arming yourselves, as you are bound to do unless you are willing to be forced into abject slavery, you are safely within the spirit and letter of the law.

The Constitution of the United States guarantees to you the right to bear arms, as it does to every other citizen, but there is not a word in this instrument, nor in any United States statute, state law, or city ordinance, that authorizes the existence of a private army for purposes of cold-blooded murder and assassination.

"Mine guard" is simply a master class term for a working class assassin.

Let the United Mine Workers and the Western Federation of Miners take note that a private army of gunmen is simply a gang of outlaws and butchers and that

THEY HAVE NOT A SOLITARY RIGHT AN HONEST WORKINGMAN IS BOUND TO RESPECT!

Let these unions and all other organized bodies of workers that are militant and not subservient to the masters, declare war to the knife on these lawless and criminal hordes and swear relentless hostility to government by gunmen in the United States.

Murderers are no less murderers because they are hired by capitalists to kill workingmen than if they were hired by workingmen to kill capitalists.

Mine guards, so-called, are murderers pure and simple, and are to be dealt with accordingly. The fact that they are in uniform, as in Colorado, makes them even more loathsome and repulsive than the common reptilian breed.

A "mine guard" in the uniform of a state militiaman is a copperhead in the skin of a rattlesnake, and possibly only because an even deadlier serpent has wriggled his slimy way into the executive chair of the state.

It remains only to be said that we stand for peace, and that we are unalterably opposed to violence and bloodshed if by any possible means, short of absolute degradation and self-abasement, these can be prevented. We believe in law, the law that applies equally to all and is impartially administered, and we prefer reason infinitely to brute force.

But when the law fails, and in fact, becomes the bulwark of crime and oppression, then an appeal to force is not only morally justified, but becomes a patriotic duty.

The Declaration of Independence proclaims this truth in words that burn with the patriotic fervor the revolutionary fathers must have felt when they rose in revolt against the red-coated gunmen of King George and resolved to shoot king rule out of existence.

Wendell Phillips declared that it was the glory of honest men to trample bad laws under foot with contempt, and it is equally their glory to protect themselves in their lawful rights when those who rule the law fail to give them such protection.

Let the unions, therefore, arm their members against the gunmen of the corporations, the gangs of criminals, cut-throats, women-ravishers and baby-burners that have absolutely no lawful right to existence!

Let organized labor, from one end of the country to the other, declare war on these privately licensed assassins, and let the slogan of every union man in the land be

DOWN WITH GOVERNMENT BY GUNMEN AND ASSASSINATION IN THE UNITED STATES!

International Socialist Review, September, 1914.

The Knights of Columbus

On a speaking tour in the middle and eastern states some time ago I was given the benefit of a line of free advertising from a new and unexpected source. It had all been prearranged and covered practically every point on the trip.

This advertising consisted of a hand-bill, placed on every doorstep the night before my arrival, warning the people against me as an infidel, the friend and defender of Gorky (who was denounced in the same circular as a moral leper), the champion of free love and the enemy of religion, morality and Christian life. In short, I was pictured as a monster going from place to place corrupting the morals of the people, undermining the fabric of society, blaspheming the church, reviling religion, breaking up the home, destroying the family, and sowing the seed of violent and bloody revolution.

This hand-bill was signed, THE KNIGHTS OF COLUMBUS. It did not bear the union label.

In some places it was supplemented by a half-page advertisement in a local paper containing substantially the same matter. At several points it was still further supplemented by the priest's warning to the faithful, issued from the pulpit, to beware, as they valued their souls, of the Socialist free-lover and home-destroyer who was about to invade the city.

Of course the effect was exactly opposite that intended. Curiosity to see the monster was aroused and could not be resisted. Instead of empty chairs the house was crowded at every point.

The experiment was abandoned as suddenly as it was undertaken. Never since have my lectures been openly advertised by the Knights of Columbus. I am still the recipient of their knightly religious and moral attention, but covertly and in the dark, and no longer by public advertisement.

On the same trip a workingman who was at the same time a Catholic and a Socialist asked me to account for the venomous hostility of the Knights of Columbus to the Socialist movement. I did not, in answering, attack or denounce the Knights of Columbus. I shall not do so now. I did, however, put a series of questions to my questioner and let him answer them for himself, with the result that he now understands as clearly as do all well-informed Socialists, as well as all well-informed Knights of Columbus, just why the Knights of

Columbus, ostensibly a social and mutual benefit association, has vaulted into the arena as the special champion of the church and religion against the alleged onslaughts of the Socialist movement.

I have had occasion to observe closely and study carefully this organization, its backers and promoters, as well as its purpose, its policy and its tactics; I have been on the trail of its agents and emissaries and could easily, were I so disposed, convict some of its leading lights of personal falsehood and slander, but I have no time for that. If they find it necessary to hurt me and help themselves in that way it is only because the truth will not serve them and I am satisfied with the compliment and willing to let it pass.

I am not going to descend to the level the Knights of Columbus found it necessary to do when it spread the report broadcast that I was a monster of meanness and depravity at a time and under circumstances when I had little or no chance to be heard in my own behalf. I am willing that it shall exhaust its entire capacity in the attempt to discredit Socialists and destroy Socialism, but I insist that it shall fly its true colors and be known to the working people for exactly what it is in its relentless warfare upon their revolutionary movement.

The vast majority of the Knights of Columbus are honest, but their minds have been methodically poisoned against Socialism. Of their own knowledge they know, and are permitted to know, little or nothing about Socialism. They have taken the word of their "superiors" for it and hence regard Socialism as an unclean, hateful thing to be resisted as religiously as if it were led by the devil himself.

To these misinformed and misguided Catholic workingmen I wish to admit in all candor that the Knights of Columbus has a sound reason and a well-defined purpose in fighting Socialism, but that it is not because Socialism is a menace to religion, or morality, or the church, or the family, or the home. That is but the pretext, the excuse behind which lurk in the dark shadow the *real reason, the true purpose* for arousing hatred against Socialists and inciting bitter opposition to the Socialist movement.

The enemies of the human race have always persecuted reformers and resisted progress in the name of religion. The scribes and pharisees (whom He denounced as hypocrites) and who conspired to have Him crucified, accused Jesus Christ of "spreading a false religion," the same charge the Knights of Columbus are repeating today in their warfare on Socialism.

But it was not on account of His alleged attack on religion, but on account of His real attack on the robbery of the poor by the rich that He was branded as a blasphemer and crucified as a convict.

"Religion" was the excuse, the subterfuge of the money-changers, the shylocks, the grinders of the poor then as it is today, to discredit the man and crush the movement that threatens the system in which the workers are robbed, impoverished and brutalized by the master class.

When Mark Hanna extolled the virtues of the Catholic Church and declared it to be the bulwark of the future it was not because he had a particle of use for the Catholic religion, but because as a captain of industry he had a keen eye for the possibilities of the Knights of Columbus.

If the members of the Knights of Columbus, the rank and file, the common herd as they are known in "upper class" circles, will persist in having the following questions truthfully answered by those of their leaders and preceptors who are in position to know the truth, they will no longer be deceived by their professed religious advisers and spiritual saviors, but they will understand the real reason, the sole and only reason, why their association is so desperately opposed to Socialism:

First. Did Mark Hanna, E. H. Harriman, John D. Rockefeller, John Pierpont Morgan, Sr., Andrew Carnegie, August Belmont, James J. Hill and other Wall Street magnates and captains of industry, all Protestants, contribute financially in support of the Knights of Columbus and to what extent?

Second. By whom were the bulk of the funds furnished for the building of the palatial K. of C. club houses which sprang up spontaneously all over the United States?

Third. How many millions of dollars is the Catholic Archbishop Ireland, boon companion of James J. Hill, the Protestant promoter, worth, and how did he acquire his great fortune?

Fourth. What interest has Wall Street in building up and patronizing the Knights of Columbus?

Fifth. How does it happen that every plutocrat, every labor exploiter, every enemy of union labor, every grinder of the faces of the poor, every devourer of widows' houses and every corrupt politician in the land is a friend of the Knights of Columbus and a foe of the Socialism movement?

Sixth. What interests have Protestant capitalists in the "religion" of Catholic wage-slaves?

Seventh. Who pays the salaries and expenses of the gentlemen who travel over the country under the auspices of the Knights of Columbus to defame Socialists and warn the faithful against the Socialist movement?

Eighth. How does it happen that the great capitalist newspapers, owned by Protestants, are so extremely friendly to the Catholic Knights of Columbus that they give columns and columns of space to the attacks made by its speakers upon Socialists and Socialism, and laud them to the skies editorially, while at the same time they either ignore the great meetings held by Socialists or deliberately misquote and malign Socialist speakers?

Ninth. Do you not think it strange that the rich who live out of your labor, who look down upon you as the low, vulgar and ignorant herd; who never associate with you or have anything in common with you, are so painfully concerned about your "religion," your "morals," and your "spiritual salvation"?

Tenth. Does it not seem a trifle unusual that the rich and respectable "upper class," who look down upon you as the "lower class"— the great majority of whom have no homes you can call your own— are so bitterly hostile to Socialism because it will break up your homes?

Eleventh. Can you account for the Knights of Columbus receiving large contributions of funds from Protestant gentlemen who, according to the Catholic religion, are heretics and therefore doomed to damnation?

Twelfth. Do you know of any Jew, outside of the Knights of Columbus, who turned Catholic from the sole desire to save the souls of the working class from Socialism and damnation?

Thirteenth. Can you think of any possible reason why Socialists, who are human beings like yourselves, would want to destroy your homes, and what they would have to gain by breaking up your families (those of you who have any), and sending your souls to purgatory?

Fourteenth. Have you ever paused to take notice that those who are so profoundly interested in having you lay up treasures in heaven have swiped about all the treasures on earth?

Fifteenth. Does it not strike you as rather remarkable that the rich war lords who declare war and have millions of you workers, Catholics and Protestants, Jews and Gentiles, white and black, fall upon and cut one another's throats—does it not seem at least a bit strange that these eminent gentlemen, all of them friends of the Knights of Columbus and all of them enemies of Socialism, should be so fearful that you workers may not get to heaven—soon enough?

Sooner or later the Catholic workingmen will know the truth and when they do they will line up, as thousands of them have already done, with all other workingmen in the Socialist movement, the movement of the working class in the world-wide conflict for the destruction of wage-slavery and the emancipation of the workers of the world.

International Socialist Review, April, 1915.

The prospect for peace

There is no doubt that the belligerent nations of Europe are all heartily sick of war and that they would all welcome peace even if they could not dictate all its terms.

But it should not be overlooked that this frightful upheaval is but a symptom of the international readjustment which the underlying economic forces are bringing about, as well as the fundamental changes which are being wrought in our industrial and political institutions. Still, every war must end and so must this. The destruction of both life and property has been so appalling during the eighteen months that the war has been waged that we may well conclude that the fury of the conflict is largely spent and that, with bankruptcy and ruin such as the world never beheld staring them in the face, the lords of capitalist misrule are about ready to sue for peace.

From the point of view of the working class, the chief sufferers in this as in every war, the most promising indication of peace is the international conference recently held in Zimmerwald, Switzerland, attended by representatives of all European neutral nations and some of the belligerent powers. This conference, consisting wholly of representatives of the working class issued a ringing manifesto in favor of international re-organization on a permanent and uncompromising anti-war basis and of putting forth all possible efforts to end the bloody conflict which for a year and a half has shocked Christendom and outraged the civilization of the world.

The manifesto above referred to has been received with enthusiasm by the workers of all of the belligerent nations and the sentiment in favor of its acceptance and of the program of procedure it lays down is spreading rapidly in labor circles in the nations at war as well as in those at peace.

It would no doubt do much to clear the situation and expedite peace overtures if a decisive battle were fought and the indications are that such a battle, or series of battles, will be fought between now and spring. But the opportune moment for pressing peace negotiations can be determined only by the logic of events and when this comes the people of the United States should be ready to help in every way in their power to terminate this unholy massacre and bring peace to the world.

As to the terms upon which peace is to be restored these will no doubt be determined mainly by the status of the several belligerent powers when the war is ended. A program of disarmament looking to the prevention of another such catastrophe would seem to be suggested by the present heart-breaking situation but as experience has demonstrated that capitalist nations have no honor and that the most solemn treaty is but a "scrap of paper" in their mad rivalry for conquest and plunder, such a program, even if adopted, might prove abortive and barren of results.

The matter of the conquered provinces will no doubt figure largely in the peace negotiations and the only way to settle that in accordance with the higher principles of civilized nations is to allow the people of each province in dispute to decide for themselves by popular vote what nation they desire to be annexed to, or to remain, if they prefer, independent sovereignties.

Permanent peace, however; peace based upon social justice, will never prevail until national industrial despotism has been supplanted by international industrial democracy. The end of profit and plunder among nations will also mean the end of war and the dawning of the era of "Peace on Earth and Good Will among Men."

American Socialist, February 19, 1916. Written for the Scripps League, containing 117 newspapers, in answer to the request for an expression of opinion as to the prospect for peace.

Politicians and preachers

"**B**irds have their nests and foxes have their holes but the Son of Man hath not where to lay his head." Capitalism has its politicians and militarism its preachers and both are fitly described in the scriptures:

"His watchmen are blind; they are all ignorant; they are dumb dogs; they cannot bark; sleeping, lying down, loving to slumber."

"Yea, they are greedy dogs, which can never have enough, and they are shepherds that cannot understand; they all look to their own way, every one for his gain, from his quarter."

The politicians and preachers of capitalism are set up as the shepherds of the flock, the politicians holding aloft the banner of patriotism and the preachers arrayed in the livery of religion.

These are the real betrayers of the people, the hypocrites that Christ denounced and for which He was crucified; the slimy, oily-tongued deceivers of their ignorant, trusting followers, who traffic in the slavery and misery of their fellow-beings that they may tread the paths of ease and bask in the favors of their masters.

"YEA, THEY ARE GREEDY DOGS, WHICH CAN NEVER HAVE ENOUGH, AND THEY ARE SHEPHERDS THAT CANNOT UNDERSTAND; THEY ALL LOOK TO THEIR OWN WAY, EVERY ONE FOR HIS GAIN, FROM HIS QUARTER."

A few days ago one of the most prominent capitalist preachers in New York City issued a frenzied appeal from his pulpit for military preparedness. This particular dog awakened just long enough to bark furiously at the command of his plutocratic master. He may not have received his thirty pieces of silver at the time; the reward of his apostasy comes in gold and flows into his capacious receptacle that connects with his master's bank vault all the year around.

Beware of capitalism's politicians and preachers! They are the lineal descendants of the hypocrites of old who all down the ages have guarded the flock in the name of patriotism and religion and secured the choicest provender and the snuggest booths for themselves by turning the sheep over to the ravages of the wolves.

Beware of the liveried hypocrites of the landlords, the usurers, the money-changers, the stock-gamblers, the exploiters, the enslavers and despoilers of the people; beware of the ruling class politicians and preachers and mercenary menials in every form who are so profoundly concerned about your "patriotism" and your "religion" and who receive their thirty pieces for warning you against Socialism because it will endanger your morality and interfere with your salvation.

American Socialist, June 24, 1916.

Ruling class robbers

Three hundred and twenty million dollars a year, or about a million dollars a day, is the amount stolen by the ruling class robbers of the capitalist system from the treasury of the United States.

How is this shameless raid on the national treasury committed? Easy enough. Most of the rich (!) men in this, as in every other country, are perjurers and thieves and if the law of their own making were enforced they would all be keeping the lockstep with the other thieves and felons in the penitentiary.

The plutocrats and their lesser breed ought to pay four hundred million dollars in income tax annually into the treasury of the United States. They actually pay but eighty million dollars of that amount. The difference, three hundred and twenty million dollars, is stolen by these rich robbers from the American people every year.

Basil M. Manly, the expert government investigator, after six months of thorough investigation, has brought this robbery to light and supported it by an array of unimpeachable facts and figures. His exposé of the rich tax-dodgers, perjurers and thieves is complete and ought to be read by every honest man in the land. The report is entitled "The United States Income Tax Steal" and is published under the direction of the Newspaper Enterprise Association, under whose direction the investigation was conducted, which has uncovered and laid bare this colossal robbery of the public treasury.

Since the gigantic steal has been exposed, Secretary McAdoo, Secretary of the Treasury, has been explaining that there is no adequate provision for enforcing the law and that therefore the tax can not be collected, nor the eminently respectable tax-dodging perjurers and thieves brought to justice. Exactly! But did any poor pilferer of a penny's worth of stale bread to allay his hunger pangs ever es-

---

cape the heavy hand of the law upon the same ground of inadequate provision to enforce its penalties?

As a matter of fact the income tax law was never intended to be enforced. Under its provisions the rich thieves are permitted to make secret returns and the law was expressly drawn to make it safe and easy for them to perjure themselves, dodge their taxes and laugh up their sleeves.

For do not these plug-hatted, tailor-made, manicured thieves and looters furnish the campaign funds of the capitalist parties that control the government? And are they not the ruling class of the nation and therefore above the law that rules the common herd?

Yes, and they are also the infernal humbugs and hypocrites that forever prate about "patriotism" and "equality before the law" and "the power of the nation."

Oh, yes, and the whole burglarizing gang of them are for "preparedness" and for making every wage-slave a soldier-hireling to defend the country against a foreign invasion.

Both the Republican and Democratic national conventions recently held were financed and controlled by these treasury-looting scoundrels, and both Hughes and Wilson are their candidates for the presidency of the United States.

We are ruled by robbers who pose as patriots and if you want the facts and figures to prove it write to S. T. Hughes, Editor, Newspaper Enterprise Association, Cleveland, O., and ask him to send you a copy of the Manly report on the United States Income Tax Steal of three hundred and twenty million dollars a year.

American Socialist, July 1, 1916.

The I. W. W. bogey

The morning paper I have just read contains an extended press dispatch from Washington, under screaming head-lines, making the startling disclosure that a world-wide con-spiracy to overthrow the existing social order has been unearthed by the secret service agents of the government. The basis of the conspiracy is reported to have been the discovery of some guns and ammunition in the hold of a Russian freighter just arrived at a Pacific port in charge of a Bolsheviki crew, from which it has been deduced that the guns must have been sent by the Russian revolu-tionists to the I. W. W. of the United States in pursuance of a con-spiracy of the Russian reds, the Sinn Fein leaders of Ireland, and the American I.W.W.'s to overthrow all governments of the civi-lized world.

This is really too much!

We are not told how the Sinn Feiners happen to get in on this universal conspiracy, but as their name, like that of the Bolsheviki and the I.W.W., has great potency as a bogey to frighten the feeble-minded, the inventors of this wonderful cock-and-bull story may well be allowed this additional license to their perfervid imagination.

Everything that happens nowadays that the ruling classes do not like and everything that does not happen that they do like is laid at the door of the I.W.W. Its name is anathema wherever capitalism wields the last and drains the being of its exploited victims.

It is a wonderful compliment! Is the working class wise to its significance? Unfortunately not or the leaders and moving spirits of this persecuted industrial organization would not now be in jail wait-ing month after month to be tried for criminal offenses charged against them which they never dreamed of committing.

I think I may claim to be fairly well informed as to the methods and tactics of the I.W.W.—with some of which I am not at all in agreement—and I have no hesitancy in branding the sweeping crimi-nal charges made against them since the war was declared as utterly false and malicious and without so much as a shadow of foundation in fact.

Repeatedly the sensational charge has been spread broadcast through the capitalist press that the I.W.W. were in conspiracy to blow up the mills and factories in the East, to burn the crops and destroy the orchards in the West, poison the springs and wells in the North, paralyze the cotton and rice industries in the South, and spread ruin and desolation everywhere for the profit and glory of the crazy Teuton Kaiser and his atrocious Junker plunderbund and the overthrow of democracy and freedom in the United States.

Was a more stupendous lie or a more stupid one ever hatched in a human brain?

Look at the I. W. W. and then at the government and the more than one hundred million people of the United States! Is the lie not apparent on the very face of this absurd and malicious charge? Would any but an idiot or madman ever dream of the slaughter and destruction of an entire nation by a comparative handful of its population? Would any but a fool be deceived by such glaringly self-evident lies and calumnies?

Oh, the ghastly joke of it all! And the stark tragedy, too, when one thinks of the many simple-minded people whose attitude of fierce hostility toward the I. W. W. and its leaders is determined by these inspired fabrications!

Why should the I. W. W., organized for the very purpose of destroying despotism and establishing democracy, go across seas to lend its aid to the most brutal autocracy on the face of the earth?

Ah, but the autocracy within our own borders know how to play upon the prejudice and credulity of the unthinking and turn them against the men who at the peril of their freedom and their very lives are battling for the liberation of the people!

It is from Wall Street, the money center of the American plutocracy, that the campaign of falsehood and slander against the I. W. W. is directed; from there that the orders are issued to raid its national and state offices, jail its leaders, break up its meetings, and tar and feather and lacerate with whips and finally lynch and assassinate its speakers and organizers.

Wall Street mortally fears the I. W. W. and its growing menace to capitalist autocracy and misrule. The very name of the I. W. W. strikes terror to Wall Street's craven soul.

But Wall Street does not fear Sammy Gompers and the A. F. of L.

Every plutocrat, every profiteering pirate, every food vulture, every exploiter of labor, every robber and oppressor of the poor, every hog under a silk tile, every vampire in human form, will tell you that the A. F. of L. under Gompers is a great and patriotic organization and that the I. W. W. under Haywood is a gang of traitors in the pay of the bloody Kaiser.

Which of these, think you, Mr. Wage-Slave, is your friend and the friend of your class?

It is interesting to note that at the very time the plutocracy and its hirelings are charging the I. W. W. with treason and cramming the jails with its members they are also driving union labor out into the desert to perish under armed vigilantes as at Bisbee and Bingham, while in the same hour their Supreme Court outlaws picketing and legalizes and protects strike-breaking as in the cases of the union miners in West Virginia and the southwestern states.

There is one thing in this situation that is clear to every union man, to every sympathizer with the working class, and every believer in justice and fair play, and that is that the hundreds of I.W.W.'s and Socialists now in jail are entitled to be fairly tried. Upon that question there can be no difference among decent men, whatever may be their attitude toward the union and its principles. The Socialist Party, through its national executive committee—to its supreme credit—has taken this position and in a ringing declaration and appeal has expressed its determination that the accused I.W.W. leaders and members receive a fair trail and a square deal.

To this end money will be needed, all that can be raised, and as the Captain Kidd Kaiser and his pirate crew of Junkers have not yet come across with that cargo of gold covering the purchase price of the I. W. W., it becomes the duty of every one who is with us to forthwith send his contribution to the defense of our shamelessly persecuted comrades.

This is our fight! We of the working class are all vitally interested in the outcome.

The war within the war and beyond the war in which the I.W.W. is fighting—the war of the workers of all countries against the exploiters of all countries—is our war, the war of humanity against its oppressors and despoilers, the holiest war ever waged since the race began.

Let there be no mistake. The guerrilla warfare of Wall Street is not against the I. W. W. alone but against the labor movement in general except in so far as union labor suffers itself to be emasculated and crawls on its belly at the feet of its despotic masters.

A spineless and apologetic union bearing the official seal of the

Civic Federation is the noblest specimen of working class patriotism in the eyes of our Wall Street rulers.

Now is the time to meet the attack; to resist the assault; to turn the guns on the real conspirators. The inevitable reaction will swiftly follow and instead of smashing the revolutionary labor movement this dastardly conspiracy will prove the making of it.

Now is the time for the fighting union men of America to stand together. The situation is the grimmest that ever confronted the working class but every such crisis bears with it the golden opportunity to the workers to strike the decisive blow and to forge ahead to a higher level of life. To take advantage of this supreme opportunity and profit by it to the limit, the workers must be united and act together like a well-disciplined army.

Solidarity must be the watchword!

As we stand upon the threshold of the year 1918 let us resolve to make it the most luminous one in the annals of proletarian achievement.

Industrial unity and political unity, the revolutionary solidarity of the working class, will give us the power to conquer capitalism and emancipate the workers of the world.

International Socialist Review, February, 1918.

The Canton, Ohio speech

Comrades, friends and fellow-workers, for this very cordial greeting, this very hearty reception, I thank you all with the fullest appreciation of your interest in and your devotion to the cause for which I am to speak to you this afternoon. (Applause.)

To speak for labor; to plead the cause of the men and women and children who toil; to serve the working class, has always been to me a high privilege; (Applause) a duty of love.

I have just returned from a visit over yonder (pointing to the workhouse), where three of our most loyal comrades[1] are paying the penalty for their devotion to the cause of the working class. (Applause.) They have come to realize, as many of us have, that it is extremely dangerous to exercise the constitutional right of free speech in a country fighting to make democracy safe in the world. (Applause.)

I realize that, in speaking to you this afternoon, there are certain limitations placed upon the right of free speech. I must be exceedingly careful, prudent, as to what I say, and even more careful and prudent as to how I say it. (Laughter.) I may not be able to say all I think; (Laughter and applause) but I am not going to say anything that I do not think. (Applause.) I would rather a thousand times be a free soul in jail than to be a sycophant and coward in the streets. (Applause and shouts.) They may put those boys in jail—and some of the rest of us in jail—but they can not put the Socialist movement in jail. (Applause and shouts.) Those prison bars separate their bodies from ours, but their souls are here this afternoon. (Applause and cheers.) They are simply paying the penalty, that all men have paid in all the ages of history, for standing erect, and for seeking to pave the way to better conditions for mankind. (Applause.)

If it had not been for the men and women, who, in the past, have had the moral courage to go to jail, we would still be in the jungles. (Applause.)

There is but one thing you have to be concerned about, and that is that you keep four-square with the principles of the international Socialist movement. (Applause.) It is only when you begin to compromise that trouble begins. (Applause.) So far as I am concerned, it

---

[1] Debs refers to three Cleveland Socialists, Charles E. Ruthenberg, Alfred Wagenknecht, and Charles Baker, imprisoned because of their opposition to the war.

does not matter what others may say, or think, or do, as long as I am sure that I am right with myself and the cause. (Applause.) There are so many who seek refuge in the popular side of a great question. As a socialist, I have long since learned how to stand alone. (Applause.)...

I never had much faith in leaders. (Laughter.) I am willing to be charged with almost anything, rather than to be charged with being a leader. I am suspicious of leaders, and especially of the intellectual variety. (Applause.) Give me the rank and file every day in the week. If you go to the city of Washington, and you examine the pages of the Congressional Directory, you will find that almost all of those corporation lawyers and cowardly politicians, members of Congress, and misrepresentatives of the masses—you will find that almost all of them claim, in glowing terms, that they have risen from the ranks to places of eminence and distinction. I am very glad I can not make that claim for myself. (Laughter.) I would be ashamed to admit that I had risen from the ranks. When I rise it will be with the ranks, and not from the ranks. (Applause.)

They who have been reading the capitalist newspapers realize what a capacity they have for lying. We have been reading them lately. They know all about the Socialist Party...except what is true. (Laughter.) Only the other day they took an article that I had written—and most of you have read it—most of you members of the party, at least—and they made it appear that I had undergone a marvelous transformation. (Laughter.) I had suddenly become changed—had in fact come to my senses; I had ceased to be a wicked Socialist, and had become a respectable Socialist, (Laughter) a patriotic Socialist—as if I had ever been anything else. (Laughter.)

What was the purpose of this deliberate misrepresentation? It is so self-evident that it suggests itself. The purpose was to sow the seeds of dissension in our ranks; to have it appear that we were divided among ourselves; that we were pitted against each other, to our mutual undoing. But Socialists were not born yesterday. (Applause.) They know how to read capitalist newspapers; (Laughter and applause) and to believe exactly the opposite of what they read. (Applause and laughter.)

Why should a Socialist be discouraged on the eve of the greatest triumph in all the history of the Socialist movement? (Applause.) It is true that these are anxious, trying days for us all—testing days for the women and men who are upholding the banner of labor in the struggle of the working class of all the world against the exploiters of all the world; (Applause) a time in which the weak and cowardly will falter and fail and desert. They lack the fibre to endure the revolutionary test; they fall away; they disappear as if they had never been. On the other hand, they who are animated by the unconquerable spirit of the social revolution; they who have the moral courage to stand erect and assert their convictions; stand by them; fight for them; go to jail or to hell for them, if need be—(Applause and shouts) they are writing their names, in this crucial hour—they are writing their names in fadeless letters in the history of mankind. (Applause.)...

Are we opposed to Prussian militarism? (Laughter.) (Shouts from the crown of "Yes, Yes!") Why, we have been fighting it since the day the Socialist movement was born; (Applause) and we are going to continue to fight it, day and night, until it is wiped from the face of the earth. (Thunderous applause and cheers.) Between us there is no truce—no compromise.

But, before I proceed along this line, let me recall a little history, in which I think we are all interested.

In 1869 that grand old warrior of the social revolution, the elder Liebknecht, was arrested and sentenced to prison for three months, because of his war, as a Socialist, on the Kaiser and on the Junkers that rule Germany. In the meantime the Franco-Prussian war broke out. Liebknecht and Bebel were the Socialist members in the Reichstag. They were the only two who had the courage to protest against taking Alsace-Lorraine from France and annexing it to Germany. And for this they were sentenced two years to a prison fortress charged with high treason; because, even in that early day, almost fifty years ago, these leaders, these forerunners of the international Socialist movement were fighting the Kaiser and fighting the Junkers of Germany. (Great applause and cheers.) They have continued to fight them from that day to this. (Applause.) Multiplied thousands of Socialists have languished in the jails of Germany because of their heroic warfare upon the despotic ruling class of that country. (Applause.)

I hate, I loathe, I despise Junkers and junkerdom. I have no earthy use for the Junkers of Germany, and not one particle more use for the Junkers in the United States. (Thunderous applause and cheers.)

They tell us that we live in a great free republic; that our institutions are democratic; that we are a free and self-governing people. (Laughter.) This is too much, even for a joke. (Laughter.) But it is not

---

a subject for levity; it is an exceedingly serious matter.

To whom do the Wall Street Junkers in our country marry their daughters? After they have wrung their countless millions from your sweat, your agony and your life's blood, in a time of war as in a time of peace, they invest these untold millions in the purchase of titles of broken-down aristocrats, such as princes, dukes, counts and other parasites and no-accounts. (Laughter.) Would they be satisfied to wed their daughters to honest workingmen? (Shouts from the crowd, "No!") To real democrats? Oh, no! They scour the markets of Europe for vampires who are titled and nothing else. (Laughter.) And they swap their millions for the titles, so that matrimony with them becomes literally a matter of money. (Laughter.)

These are the gentry who are today wrapped up in the American flag, who shout their claim from the housetops that they are the only patriots, and who have their magnifying glasses in hand, scanning the country for evidence of disloyalty, eager to apply the brand of treason to the men who dare to even whisper their opposition to junker rule in the United States. No wonder Sam Johnson declared that "patriotism is the last refuge of the scoundrel." He must have had this Wall Street gentry in mind, or at least their prototypes, for in every age it has been the tyrant, the oppressor and the exploiter who has wrapped himself in the cloak of patriotism, or religion, or both to deceive and overawe the people. (Applause.)

I know Tom Mooney intimately—as if he were my own brother. He is an absolutely honest man. (Applause.) He had no more to do with the crime with which he was charged and for which he was convicted than I had. (Applause.) And if he ought to go to the gallows, so ought I. If he is guilty every man who belongs to a labor organization or to the Socialist Party is likewise guilty.

What is Tom Mooney guilty of? I will tell you. I am familiar with his record. For years he has been fighting bravely and without compromise the battles of the working class out on the Pacific coast. He refused to be bribed and he could not be browbeaten. In spite of all attempts to intimidate him he continued loyally in the service of the organized workers, and for this he became a marked man. The henchmen of the powerful and corrupt corporations, concluding finally that he could not be bought or bribed or bullied, decided he must therefore be murdered. That is why Tom Mooney is today a life prisoner, and why he would have been hanged as a felon long years ago but for the world-wide protest of the working class. (Applause.)

Who appoints our federal judges? The people? In all the history of the country, the working class have never named a federal judge. There are 121 of these judges and every solitary one holds his position, his tenure, through the influence and power of corporate when they go to the bench, they go, not to serve the people, but to serve the interests that place them and keep them where they are.

Why, the other day, by a vote of five to four—a kind of craps game—(Laughter) come seven, come even—(Laughter) they declared the child labor law unconstitutional—a law secured after twenty years of education and agitation on the part of all kinds of corporation lawyers, with just one exception, wiped that law from the statute books, and this in our so-called Democracy, so that we may continue to grind the flesh and blood and bones of puny little children into profits for the junkers of Wall Street. (Applause.) And this in a country that boasts of fighting to make the world safe for democracy! (Laughter.) The history of this country is being written in the blood of the childhoods the industrial lords have murdered.

How stupid and short-sighted the ruling class really is! Cupidity is stone blind. It has no vision. The greedy, profit-seeking exploiter cannot see beyond the end of his nose. He can see a chance for an "opening"; he is cunning enough to know what graft is and where it is, and how it can be secured, but vision he has none—not the slightest. He knows nothing of the great throbbing world that spreads out in all directions. He has no capacity for literature; no appreciation of art; no soul for beauty. That is the penalty the parasites pay for the violation of the laws of life... Every move they make in their game of greed but hastens their own doom. Every blow they strike at the Socialist movement reacts upon themselves. Every time they strike at us, they hit themselves. It never fails. (Applause.) Every time they strangle a Socialist paper they add a thousand voices proclaiming the truth of the principles of Socialism and the ideals of the Socialist movement. They help us in spite of themselves.

Socialism is a growing idea; an expanding philosophy. It is spreading over the entire face of the earth. It is as vain to resist it as it would be to arrest the sunrise on the morrow. It is coming, coming, coming all along the line. Can you not see it? If not, I advise you to consult an oculist. There is certainly something the matter with your vision. It is the mightiest movement in the history of mankind. What a privilege

---

to serve it? I have regretted a thousand times that I can do so little for the movement that has done so much for me. (Applause.) The little that I am, the little that I am hoping to be, I owe to the Socialist movement. (Applause.) It has given me my ideas and ideals; my principles and convictions, and I would not exchange one of them for all of Rockefeller's blood-stained dollars. (Cheers.) It has taught me how to serve—a lesson to me of priceless value. It has taught me the ecstasy in the handclasp of a comrade. It has enabled me to hold high communion with you, and made it possible for me to take my place side by side with you in the great struggle for the better day; to multiply myself over and over again; to thrill with a fresh born manhood; to feel life truly worth while; to open new avenues of vision; to spread out glorious vistas; to know that I am kin to all that throbs; to be class-conscious, and to realize that, regardless of nationality, race, creed, color or sex, every man, every woman who toils, who renders useful service, every member of the working class without an exception, is my comrade, my brother and sister—and that to serve them and their cause is the highest duty of my life. (Great applause.)

Yes, my comrades, my heart is attuned to yours. Aye, all our hearts now throb as one great heart responsive to the battle-cry of the social revolution. Here, in this alert and inspiring assemblage (Applause) our hearts are with the Bolsheviki of Russia. (Deafening and prolonged applause.) Those heroic men and women, those unconquerable comrades have by their incomparable valor and sacrifice added fresh lustre to the fame of the international movement...The very first act of the triumphant Russian revolution was to proclaim a state of peace with all mankind, coupled with a fervent moral appeal, not to kings, not to emperors, rulers of diplomats but to *the people* of all nations ...When the Bolsheviki came into power and went through the archives they found and exposed the secret treaties—the treaties that were made between the Czar and the French Government, the British Government and the Italian Government, proposing, after the victory was achieved, to dismember the German Empire and destroy the Central Powers. These treaties have never been denied nor repudiated. Very little has been said about them in the American press. I have a copy of these treaties, showing the purpose of the Allies is exactly the purpose of the Central Powers, and that is the conquest and spoliation of the weaker nations that has always been the purpose of war.

Wars throughout history have been waged for conquest and plunder. In the Middle Ages when the feudal lords who inhabited the castles whose towers may still be seen along the Rhine concluded to enlarge their domains, to increase their power, their prestige and their wealth they declared war upon one another. But they themselves did not go to war any more than the modern feudal lords, the barons of Wall Street go to war. (Applause.) The feudal barons of the Middle Ages, the economic predecessors of the capitalists of our day, declared all wars. And their miserable serfs fought all the battles. The poor, ignorant serfs had been taught to revere their masters; to believe that when their masters declared war upon one another, it was their patriotic duty to fall upon one another and to cut one another's throats for the profit and glory of the lords and barons who held them in contempt. And that is war in a nutshell. The master class has always declared the wars; the subject class has always fought the battles. The master class has had all to gain and nothing to lose, while the subject class has had nothing to gain and all to lose—especially their lives. (Applause.)

And here let me emphasize the fact—and it cannot be repeated too often—that the working class who fight all the battles, the working class who make the supreme sacrifices, the working class who freely shed their blood and furnish the corpses, have never yet had a voice in either declaring war or making peace. It is the ruling class that invariably does both. They alone declare war and they alone make peace.

"Yours not to reason why;
Yours but to do or die."

That is their motto and we object on the part of the awakening workers of this nation...

What a compliment it is to the Socialist movement to be persecuted for the sake of the truth! The truth alone will make the people free. (Applause.) And for this reason the truth must not be permitted to reach the people. The truth has always been dangerous to the rule of the rogue, the exploiter, the robber. So the truth must be ruthlessly suppressed. That is why they are trying to destroy the Socialist movement; and every time they strike a blow they add a thousand new voices to the hosts proclaiming that Socialism is the hope of humanity and has come to emancipate the people from their final form of servitude. (Applause.)

We do not attack individuals. We do not seek to avenge ourselves upon those opposed to our faith. We have no fight with individuals as such. We are capable of pitying those who hate us. (Applause.) We do not hate them; we know better; we would freely give them a cup of water if they needed it. (Applause.) There is no room in our hearts for hate, except for the system, the social system in which it is possible for one man to amass a stupendous fortune doing nothing, while millions of others suffer and struggle and agonize and die for the bare necessities of existence. (Applause.)

It is the minorities who have made the history of this world. It is the few who have had the courage to take their places at the front; who have been true enough to themselves to speak the truth that was in them; who have dared oppose the established order of things; who have espoused the cause of the suffering, struggling poor; who have upheld without regard to personal consequences the cause of freedom and righteousness. It is they, the heroic, self-sacrificing few who have made the history of the race and who have paved the way from barbarism to civilization. The many prefer to remain upon the popular side. They lack the courage and vision to join a despised minority that stands for a principle; they have not the moral fibre that withstands, endures and finally conquers. They are to be pitied and not treated with contempt for they cannot help their cowardice. But, thank God, in every age and in every nation there have been the brave and self-reliant few, and they have been sufficient to their historic task; and we, who are here today, are under infinite obligations to them because they suffered, they sacrificed, they went to jail, they had their bones broken upon the wheel, they were burned at the stake and their ashes scattered to the winds by the hands of hate and revenge in their struggle to leave the world better for us than they found it for themselves. We are under eternal obligations to them because of what they did and what they suffered for us and the only way we can discharge that obligation is by doing the best we can for those who are to come after us. (Applause.)

The heart of the International Socialist never beats a retreat. (Applause.)

They are pressing forward, here, there and everywhere, in all the zones that girdle the globe. Everywhere these awakening workers, these class-conscious proletarians, these hardy sons and daughters of honest toil are proclaiming the glad tidings of the coming emancipation; everywhere their hearts are attuned to the most sacred cause that ever challenged men and women to action in all the history of the world. Everywhere they are moving toward democracy and the dawn; marching toward the sunrise, their faces all aglow with the light of the coming day. These are the Socialists, the most zealous and enthusiastic crusaders the world has ever known. (Applause.) They are making history that will light up the horizon of coming generations, for their mission is the emancipation of the human race. They have been reviled; they have been ridiculed, persecuted, imprisoned and have suffered death, but they have been sufficient to themselves and their cause, and their final triumph is but a question of time.

Do you wish to hasten the day of victory? Join the Socialist Party! Don't wait for the morrow. Join now! (Applause.) Enroll your name without fear and take your place where you belong. You cannot do your duty by proxy. You have got to do it yourself and do it squarely and then as you look yourself in the face you will have no occasion to blush. You will know what it is to be a real *man* or *woman*. You will lose nothing; you will gain everything. (Applause.) Not only will you lose nothing but you will find something of infinite value, and that something will be yourself. And that is your supreme need—to find yourself—to really know yourself and your purpose in life. (Applause.)

You need to know that it is your duty to rise above the animal plane of existence. You need to know that it is for you to know something about literature and science and art. You need to know that you are verging on the edge of a great new world. You need to get in touch with your comrades and fellow-workers and to become conscious of your interests, your powers and your possibilities as a class. You need to know that you belong to the great majority of mankind. You need to know that as long as you are ignorant, as long as you are indifferent, as long as you are apathetic, unorganized and content, you will remain exactly where you are. (Applause.) You will be exploited; you will be degraded, and you will have to beg for a job. You will get just enough for your slavish toil to keep you in working order, and you will be looked down upon with scorn and contempt by the very parasites that live and luxuriate out of your sweat and unpaid labor.

If you would be respected you have got to begin by respecting yourself. (Applause.) Stand up squarely and look yourself in the face and see a man! Do not allow yourself to fall into the predicament of the poor fellow who, after he had heard a Socialist speech concluded that he too ought to be a Socialist. The argument he had heard was unanswerable. "Yes," he said to himself, "all the speaker said was true and I certainly ought to join the party." But after a while he allowed his ardor to cool and he soberly concluded that by joining the party he might anger his boss and lose his job. He then concluded: "I can't take the chance." That night he slept alone. There was something on his conscience and it resulted in a dreadful dream. Men always have such dreams when they betray themselves. A Socialist is free to go to bed with a clear conscience. He goes to sleep with his manhood and he awakens and walks forth in the morning with his self-respect. He is unafraid and he can look the whole world in the face (Applause and laughter) without a tremor and without a blush. But this poor weakling who lacked the courage to do the bidding of his reason and conscience was haunted by a startling dream and at midnight he awoke in terror, bounded from his bed and exclaimed: "My God, there is nobody in this room." (Laughter.) He was absolutely right. (Laughter and applause.) There was nobody in that room.

How would you like to sleep in a room that had nobody in it? (Laughter.) It is an awful thing to be nobody. That is certainly a state of mind to get out of, the sooner the better...

To turn your back on the corrupt Republican Party and the corrupt Democratic Party—the gold-dust lackeys of the ruling class (Laughter.) counts for something. It counts for still more after you have stepped out of those popular and corrupt capitalist parties to join a minority party that has an ideal, that stands for a principle, and fights for a cause. (Applause.) This will be the most important change you have ever made and the time will come when you will thank me for having made the suggestion. It was the day of days for me. I remember it well. It was like passing from midnight darkness to the noontide light of day. It came almost like a flash and found me ready. It must have been in such a flash that great, seething, throbbing Russia, prepared by centuries of slavery and tears and martyrdom, was transformed from a dark continent to a land of living light.

There is something splendid, something sustaining and inspiring in the prompting of the heart to be true to yourself and to the best you know, especially in a crucial hour of your life. You are in the crucible today, my Socialist comrades! You are going to be tried by fire, to what extent no one knows. If you are weak-fibred and faint-hearted you will be lost to the Socialist movement. We will have to bid you good-bye. You are not the stuff of which revolutions are made. We are sorry for you (Applause.) unless you chance to be an "intellectual." The "intellectuals," many of them, are already gone. No loss on our side nor gain on the other.

I am always amused in the discussion of the "intellectual" phase of this question. It is the same old standard under which the rank and file are judged. What would become of the sheep if they had no shepherd to lead them out of the wilderness into the land of milk and honey?

Oh, yes, "I am your shepherd and ye are my mutton." (Laughter.)

They would have us believe that if we had no "intellectuals" we would have no movement. They would have our party, the rank and file, controlled by the "intellectual" bosses as the Republican and Democratic parties are controlled. These capitalist parties are managed by "intellectual" leaders and the rank and file are sheep that follow the bellwether to the shambles . . .

The capitalist system affects to have great regard and reward for intellect, and the capitalists give themselves full credit for having superior brains. When we have ventured to say that the time would come when the working class would rule they have bluntly answered "Never! It requires brains to rule." The workers of course have none. And they certainly try hard to prove it by proudly supporting the political parties of their masters under whose administration they are kept in poverty and servitude . . .

It is true that they have the brains that indicates the cunning of the fox, the wolf, but as for brains denoting real intelligence and the measure of intellectual capacity they are the most woefully ignorant people on earth. Give me a hundred capitalists and let me ask them a dozen simple questions about the history of their own country and I will prove to you that they are as ignorant and unlettered as any you may find in the so-called lower class. (Applause.) They know little of history; they are strangers to science; they are ignorant of sociology and blind to art but they know how to exploit, how to gouge, how to rob, and do it with legal sanction. They always proceed legally for the reason that the class which has the power to rob upon a large scale has also the power to control the government and legalize their robbery. I regret that lack of time prevents me from discussing this phase of the question more at length.

They are continually talking about your patriotic duty. It is not *their* but *your* patriotic duty that they are concerned about. There is a decided difference. Their patriotic duty never takes them to the firing line or chucks them into the trenches.

And now among other things they are urging you to "cultivate" war gardens, while at the same time a government war report just issued shows that practically 52 percent of the arable, tillable soil is held out of use by the landlords, speculators and profiteers. They themselves do not cultivate the soil. They could not if they would. Nor do they allow others to cultivate it. They keep it idle to enrich themselves, to pocket the millions of dollars of unearned increment. Who is it that makes this land valuable while it is fenced in and kept out of use? It is the people. Who pockets this tremendous accumulation of value? The landlords. And these landlords who toil not and spin not are supreme among American "patriots."

In passing I suggest that we stop a moment to think about the term "landlord." "LANDORD!" Lord of the Land! The Lord of the land is indeed a super-patriot. This lord who practically owns the earth tells you that we are fighting this war to make the world safe for democracy—he, who shuts out all humanity from his private domain; he who profiteers at the expense of the people who have been slain and mutilated by multiplied thousands, under pretense of being the great American patriot. It is he, this identical patriot who is in fact the arch-enemy of the people; it is he that you need to wipe from power. It is he who is a far greater menace to your liberty and your well-being than the Prussian junkers on the other side of the Atlantic Ocean. (Applause.)

Fifty-two percent of the land kept out of use, according to their own figures! They tell you that there is an alarming shortage of flour and that you need to produce more. They tell you further that you have got to save wheat so that more can be exported for the soldiers who are fighting on the other side, while half of your tillable soil is held out of use by the landlords and profiteers. What do you think of that?...

Let us illustrate a vital point. Here is the coal in great deposits all about us; here are the miners and the machinery of production. Why should there be a coal famine upon the one hand and an army of idle and hungry miners on the other hand? Is it not an incredibly stupid situation, an almost idiotic if not criminal state of affairs?

In the present system the miner, a wage-slave, gets down into a pit three or four hundred feet deep. He works hard and produces a ton of coal. But he does not own an ounce of it. That coal belongs to some mine-owning plutocrat who may be in New York or sailing the high seas in his private yacht; or he may be hobnobbing with royalty in the capitals of Europe, and that is where most of them were before the war was declared. The industrial captain, so-called, who lives in Paris, London, Vienna or some other center of gayety does not have to work to revel in luxury. He owns the mines and he might as well own the miners.

That is where you workers are and where you will remain as long as you give your support to the political parties of your masters and exploiters. You vote these miners out of a job and reduce them to corporation vassals and paupers.

We Socialists say: "Take possession of the mines in the name of the people." (Applause.) Set the miners at work and give every miner the equivalent of all the coal he produces. Reduce the work day in proportion to the development of productive machinery. That would at once settle the matter of a coal famine and of idle miners. But that is too simple a proposition and the people will have none of it. The time will come, however, when the people will be driven to take such action for there is no other efficient and permanent solution of the problem...

Of course that would be Socialism as far as it goes. But you are not in favor of that program. It is too visionary because it is so simple and practical. So you will have to continue to wait until winter is upon you before you get your coal and then pay three prices for it because you insist upon voting a capitalist ticket and giving your support to the present wage-slave system. The trouble with you is that you are still in a capitalist state of mind.

Lincoln said: "If you want that thing, that is the thing you want"; and you will get it to your heart's content. But some good day you will wake up and realize that a change is needed and wonder why you did not know it long before. Yes, a change is certainly needed, not merely a change of party but a change of system; a change from slavery to freedom and from despotism to democracy, wide as the world. (Applause.) When this change comes at last, we shall rise from brutehood to brotherhood, and to accomplish it we have to educate and organize the workers industrially and politically . . .

There are few men who have the courage to say a word in the favor of the I. W. W. (Applause.) I have. (Applause.) Let me say here that I have great respect for the I. W. W. Far greater than I have for their infamous detractors. (Applause.)

It is only necessary to label a man "I. W. W." to have him lynched. War makes possible all such crimes and outrages. And war comes in spite of the people. When Wall Street says war the press says war and the pulpit promptly follows with its *Amen*. In every age the pulpit has been on the side of the rulers and not on the side of the people. That is one reason why the preachers so fiercely denounce the I. W. W....

Political action and industrial action must supplement and sustain each other. You will never vote the Socialist republic into existence. You will have to lay its foundations in industrial organization. The industrial union is the forerunner of industrial democracy. In the shop where the workers are associated is where industrial democracy has its beginning. Organize according to your industries! Get together in every department of industrial service! United and acting together for the common good your power is invincible.

When you have organized industrially you will soon learn that you can manage as well as operate industry. You will soon realize that you do not need the idle masters and exploiters. They are simply parasites. They do not employ you as you imagine but you employ them to take from you what you produce, and that is how they function in industry. You can certainly dispense with them in that capacity. You do not need them to depend upon for your jobs. You can never be free while you work and live by their sufferance. You must own your own tools and then you will control your own jobs, enjoy the products of your own labor and be free men instead of industrial slaves.

Organize industrially and make your organization complete. Then unite in the Socialist Party. Vote as you strike and strike as you vote.

Your union and your party embrace the working class. The Socialist Party expresses the interest, hopes and aspirations of the toilers of all the world.

Get your fellow-workers into the industrial union and the political party to which they rightfully belong, especially this year, this historic year in which the forces of labor will assert themselves as they never have before. This is the year that calls for men and women who have the courage, the manhood and womanhood to do their duty.

Get into the Socialist Party and take your place in its ranks; help to inspire the weak and strengthen the faltering, and do your share to speed the coming of the brighter and better day for us all. (Applause.)

When we unite and act together on the industrial field and when we vote together on election day we shall develop the supreme power of the one class that can and will bring permanent peace to the world. We shall then have the intelligence, the courage and the power for our great task. In due time industry will be organized on a co-operative basis. We shall conquer the public power. We shall then transfer the title deeds of the railroads, the telegraph lines, the mines, mills and great industries to the people in their collective capacity; we shall take possession of all these social utilities in the name of the people. We shall then have industrial democracy. We shall be a free nation whose government is of and by and for the people.

And now for all of us to do our duty! The clarion call is ringing in our ears and we cannot falter without being convicted of treason to ourselves and to our great cause.

Do not worry over the charge of treason to your masters, but be concerned about the treason that involves yourselves. (Applause.) Be true to yourself and you cannot be a traitor to any good cause on earth.

Yes, in good time we are going to sweep into power in this nation and throughout the world. We are going to destroy all enslaving and degrading capitalist institutions and re-create them as free and humanizing institutions. The world is daily changing before our eyes. The sun of capitalism is setting; the sun of Socialism is rising. It is our duty to build the new nation and the free republic. We need industrial and social builders. We Socialists are the builders of the beautiful world that is to be. We are all pledged to do our part. We are inviting—aye challenging you in the name of your own manhood and womanhood to join us and do your part.

In due time the hour will strike and this great cause triumphant—the greatest in history—will proclaim the emancipation of the working class and the brotherhood of all mankind. (Thunderous and prolonged applause.)

Delivered at Nimisilla Park, Canton, Ohio, Sunday afternoon, June 16th, 1918. This speech as printed is an abridgment of the original. Omissions consist of local and out-of-date references and repetitions.

Address to the jury

Gentlemen, I do not fear to face you in this hour of accusation, nor do I shrink from the consequences of my utterances or my acts. Standing before you, charged as I am with crime, I can yet look the court in the face, I can look you in the face, I can look the world in the face, for in my conscience, in my soul, there is festering no accusation of guilt....

I wish to admit the truth of all that has been testified to in this proceeding. I have no disposition to deny anything that is true. I would not, if I could, escape the results of an adverse verdict. I would not retract a word that I have uttered that I believe to be true to save myself from going to the penitentiary for the rest of my days.

Gentlemen, you have heard the report of my speech at Canton on June 16th, and I submit that there is not a word in that speech to warrant the charges set out in the indictment. I admit having delivered the speech. I admit the accuracy of the speech in all its main features as reported in this proceeding.

In what I had to say there my purpose was to have the people understand something about the social system in which we live and to prepare them to change this system by perfectly peaceable and orderly means into what I, as a Socialist, conceive to be a real democracy.

From what you heard in the address of the counsel for the prosecution, you might naturally infer that I am an advocate of force and violence. It is not true. I have never advocated violence in any form. I have always believed in education, in intelligence, in enlightenment, and I have always made my appeal to the reason and to the conscience of the people.

I admit being opposed to the present social system. I am doing what little I can, and have been for many years, to bring about a change that shall do away with the rule of the great body of the people by a relatively small class and establish in this country an industrial and social democracy.

When great changes occur in history, when great principles are involved, as a rule the majority are wrong. The minority are usually right. In every age there have been a few heroic souls who have been in advance of their time, who have been misunderstood, maligned, persecuted, sometimes put to death. Long after their martyrdom monuments were erected to them and garlands woven from their graves . . .

A century and a half ago when the American colonists were still foreign subjects; when there were a few men who had faith in the common people and their destiny, and believed that they could rule themselves without a king; in that day to question the divine right of the king to rule was treason. If you will read Bancroft or any other American historian, you will find that a great majority of the colonists were loyal to the king and actually believed that he had a divine right to rule over them . . . But there were a few men in that day who said, "We don't need a king; we can govern ourselves." And they began an agitation that has immortalized them in history.

Washington, Jefferson, Franklin, Paine and their compeers were the rebels of their day. When they began to chafe under the rule of a foreign king and to sow the seed of resistance among the colonists they were opposed by the people and denounced by the press . . . But they had the moral courage to be true to their convictions, to stand erect and defy all the forces of reaction and detraction; and that is why their names shine in history, and why the great respectable majority of their day sleep in forgotten graves . . .

It was my good fortune to personally know Wendell Phillips. I heard the story of his cruel and cowardly persecution from his own eloquent lips just a little while before they were silenced in death.

William Lloyd Garrison, Wendell Phillips, Elizabeth Cady Stanton, Susan B. Anthony, Gerrit Smith, Thaddeus Stevens and other leaders of the Abolition movement who were regarded as public enemies and treated accordingly, were true to their faith and stood their ground. They are all in history. You are now teaching your children to revere their memories, while all of their detractors are in oblivion.

Chattel slavery has disappeared. But we are not yet free. We are engaged today in another mighty agitation. It is as wide as the world. It means the rise of the toiling masses who are gradually becoming conscious of their interests, their power, and their mission as a class; who are organizing industrially and politically and who are slowly but surely developing the economic and political power that is to set them free . . .

From the beginning of the war to this day I have never by word or act been guilty of the charged embraced in this indictment. If I have criticized, if I have condemned, it is because I believed it to be my duty, and that it was my right to do so under the laws of the land, I have had ample precedents for my attitude. This country has been engaged in a number of wars and every one of them has been condemned by some of the people, among them some of the most eminent men of their time . . .

The revolutionary fathers who had been oppressed under king's rule understood that free speech, a free press and the right of free assemblage by the people were fundamental principles in democratic government. The very first amendment to the Constitution reads:

"Congress shall make no law respecting an establishment of religion, or prohibiting the free exercise thereof; or abridging the freedom of speech, or of the press; or the right of the people peaceably to assemble, and to petition the government for a redress of grievances."

That is perfectly plain English. It can be understood by a child. I believe the revolutionary fathers meant just what is here stated—that Congress shall make no law abridging the freedom of speech or of the press, or of the right of the people to peaceably assemble, and to petition the government for a redress of their grievances.

That is the right I exercised at Canton on the 16th day of last June; and for the exercise of that right, I now have to answer to this indictment. I believe in the right of free speech, in war as well as in peace. I would not under any circumstances gag the lips of my bitterest enemy. I would under no circumstances suppress free speech. It is far more dangerous to attempt to gag the people than to allow them to speak freely what is in their hearts.

I have told you that I am no lawyer, but it seems to me that I know enough to know that if Congress enacts any law that conflicts with this provision in the Constitution, that law is void. If the Espionage Law finally stands, then the Constitution of the United States is dead....

I cannot take back a word I have said. I cannot repudiate a sentence I have uttered. I stand before you guilty of having made this speech. I do not know, I cannot tell, what your verdict may be; nor does it matter much, so far as I am concerned.

I am the smallest part of this trial. I have lived long enough to realize my own personal insignificance in relation to a great issue that involves the welfare of the whole people. What you may choose to do to me will be of small consequence after all. I am not on trial here. There is an infinitely greater issue that is being tried today in this court, though you may not be conscious of it. American institutions are on trial here before a court of American citizens. The future will render the final verdict.

And now, your honor, permit me to return my thanks for your patient consideration. And to you, gentlemen of the jury, for the kindness with which you have listened to me.

I am prepared for your verdict.

[On September 12th, 1918, Debs was convicted of having violated the Espionage Law in a speech delivered at Canton. On September 14th, he was sentenced to ten years in prison. At the close of the Government's case, Debs refused to allow any witnesses to be put on in his defense and through his chief counsel, Stedman, announced that he would plead his own cause to the jury. The case was appealed to the Supreme Court to test the constitutionality of the Espionage Law under which the indictment was returned. Debs lost his appeal.]

Statement to the court

Your Honor, years ago I recognized my kinship with all living beings, and I made up my mind that I was not one bit better than the meanest on earth, I said then, and I say now, that while there is a lower class, I am in it, while there is a criminal element I am of it, and while there is a soul in prison, I am not free.

I listened to all that was said in this court in support and justification of this prosecution, but my mind remains unchanged. I look upon the Espionage Law as a despotic enactment in flagrant conflict with democratic principles and with the spirit of free institutions...

Your Honor, I have stated in this court that I am opposed to the social system in which we live; that I believe in a fundamental change—but if possible by peaceable and orderly means...

Standing here this morning, I recall my boyhood. At fourteen I went to work in a railroad shop; at sixteen I was firing a freight engine on a railroad. I remember all the hardships and privations of that earlier day, and from that time until now my heart has been with the working class. I could have been in Congress long ago. I have preferred to go to prison...

I am thinking this morning of the men in the mills and factories; of the men in the mines and on the railroads. I am thinking of the women who for a paltry wage are compelled to work out their barren lives; of the little children who in this system are robbed of their childhood and in their tender years are seized in the remorseless grasp of Mammon and forced into the industrial dungeons, there to feed the monster machines while they themselves are being starved and stunted, body and soul. I see them dwarfed and diseased and their little lives broken and blasted because in this high noon of our twentieth-century Christian civilization money is still so much more important than the flesh and blood of childhood. In very truth gold is god today and rules with pitiless sway in the affairs of men.

In this country—the most favored beneath the bending skies—we have vast areas of the richest and most fertile soil, material resources in inexhaustible abundance, the most marvelous productive machinery on earth, and millions of eager workers ready to apply their labor to that machinery to produce in abundance for every man, woman and child—and if there are still vast numbers of our people who are the victims of poverty and whose lives are an unceasing struggle all

the way from youth to old age, until at last death comes to their rescue and stills their aching hearts and lulls these hapless victims to
dreamless sleep, it is not the fault of the Almighty: it cannot be charged
to nature, but it is due entirely to the outgrown social system in which
we live that ought to be abolished not only in the interest of the
toiling masses but in the higher interest of all humanity . . .

I believe, Your Honor, in common with all Socialists, that this
nation ought to own and control its own industries. I believe, as all
Socialists do, that all things that are jointly needed and used ought to
be jointly owned—that industry, the basis of our social life, instead of
being the private property of the few and operated for their enrich-
ment, ought to be the common property of all, democratically administered in the interest of all . . .

I am opposing a social order in which it is possible for one man
who does absolutely nothing that is useful, to amass a fortune of hundreds of millions of dollars, while millions of men and women who
work all the days of their lives secure barely enough for a wretched
existence.

This order of things cannot always endure. I have registered my
protest against it. I recognize the feebleness of my effort, but, fortunately, I am not alone. There are multiplied thousands of others who,
like myself, have come to realize that before we may truly enjoy the
blessings of civilized life, we must reorganize society upon a mutual
and co-operative basis; and to this end we have organized a great
economic and political movement that spreads over the face of all
the earth.

There are today upwards of sixty millions of Socialists, loyal, devoted adherents to this cause, regardless of nationality, race, creed,
color or sex. They are all making common cause. They are spreading with tireless energy the propaganda of the new social order. They
are waiting, watching and working hopefully through all the hours of
the day and the night. They are still in a minority. But they have
learned how to be patient and to bide their time. They feel—they
know, indeed—that the time is coming, in spite of all opposition, all
persecution, when this emancipating gospel will spread among all
the peoples, and when this minority will become the triumphant
majority and, sweeping into power, inaugurate the greatest social
and economic change in history.

In that day we shall have the universal commonwealth—the har-

---

monious co-operation of every nation with every other nation on earth . . .

Your Honor, I ask no mercy and I plead for no immunity. I realize that finally the right must prevail. I never so clearly comprehended as now the great struggle between the powers of greed and exploitation on the one hand and upon the other the rising hosts of industrial freedom and social justice.

I can see the dawn of the better day for humanity. The people are awakening. In due time they will and must come to their own.

"When the mariner, sailing over tropic seas, looks for relief from his weary watch, he turns his eyes toward the southern cross, burning luridly above the tempest-vexed ocean. As the midnight approaches, the southern cross begins to bend, the whirling worlds change their places, and with starry finger-points the Almighty marks the passage of time upon the dial of the universe, and though no bell may beat the glad tidings, the lookout knows that the midnight is passing and that relief and rest are close at hand.

"Let the people everywhere take heart of hope, for the cross is bending, the midnight is passing, and joy cometh with the morning."

"He's true to God who's true to man; wherever wrong is done,
To the humblest and the weakest, 'neath the all-beholding sun.
That wrong is done to us, and they are slaves most base,
Whose love of right is for themselves and not for all the race."

I am now prepared to receive your sentence.

The day of the people

U pon his release from the Kaiser's bastille—the doors of which were torn from their hinges by the proletarian revolution— Karl Liebknecht, heroic leader of the rising hosts, exclaimed: "The Day of the People has arrived!" It was a magnificent challenge to the Junkers and an inspiring battle-cry to the aroused workers.

From that day to this Liebknecht, Rosa Luxemburg and other true leaders of the German proletariat have stood bravely at the front, appealing to the workers to join the revolution and make it complete by destroying what remained of the criminal and corrupt old regime and ushering in the day of the people. Then arose the cry that the people were not yet ready for their day, and Ebert and Scheidemann and their crowd of white-livered reactionaries, with the sanction and support of the fugitive Kaiser, the infamous Junkers and all the Allied powers, now in beautiful alliance, proceeded to prove that the people were not yet ready to rule themselves by setting up a bourgeois government under which the working class should remain in substantially the same state of slavish subjection they were in at the beginning of the war.

And now upon that issue—as to whether the terrible war has brought the people their day or whether its appalling sacrifices have all been in vain—the battle is raging in Germany as in Russia, and the near future will determine whether revolution has for once been really triumphant or whether sudden reaction has again won the day.

In the struggle in Russia the revolution has thus far triumphed for the reason that it has not compromised. The career of Kerensky was cut short when he attempted to turn the revolutionary tide into reactionary bourgeois channels.

Lenin and Trotsky were the men of the hour and under their fearless, incorruptible and uncompromising leadership the Russian proletariat has held the fort against the combined assaults of all the ruling class powers of earth. It is a magnificent spectacle. It stirs the blood and warms the heart of every revolutionist, and it challenges the admiration of all the world.

So far as the Russian proletariat is concerned, the day of the people has arrived, and they are fighting and dying as only heroes and martyrs can fight and die to usher in the day of the people not only in Russia but in all the nations on the globe.

In every revolution of the past the false and cowardly plea that

---

the people were "not yet ready" has prevailed. Some intermediate class invariably supplanted the class that was overthrown and "the people" remained at the bottom where they have been since the beginning of history. They have never been "ready" to rid themselves of their despots, robbers and parasites. All they have ever been ready for has been to exchange one brood of vampires for another to drain their being and fatten on their misery.

That was Kerensky's doctrine in Russia and it is Scheidemann's doctrine in Germany. They are both false prophets of the people and traitors to the working class, and woe be to their deluded followers if their vicious reaction triumphs, for then indeed will the yokes be fastened afresh upon their scarred and bleeding necks for another generation.

When Kerensky attempted to side-track the revolution in Russia by joining forces with the bourgeoisie he was lauded by the capitalist press of the whole world. When Scheidemann patriotically rushed to the support of the Kaiser and the Junkers at the beginning of the war, the same press denounced him as the betrayer of Socialism and the enemy of the people. And now this very press lauds him to the heavens as the savior of the German nation! Think of it! Scheidemann the traitor has become Scheidemann the hero of the bourgeoisie. Could it be for any other reason on earth than that Scheidemann is doing the dirty work of the capitalist class?

And all this time the prostitute press of the robber regime of the whole world is shrieking hideously against Bolshevism. "It is worse than Kaiserism" is the burden of their cry. Certainly it is. They would a thousand times rather have the Kaiser restored to his throne than to see the working class rise to power. In the latter event they cease to rule, their graft is gone and their class disappears, and well do they know it. That is what we said from the beginning and for which we have been sentenced as disloyalists and traitors.

Scheidemann and his breed do not believe that the day of the people has arrived. According to them the war and the revolution have brought the day of the bourgeoisie. Mr. Bourgeois is now to take the place of Mr. Junker—to evolute into another Junker himself by and by—while Mr. Wage-Slave remains where he was before, under the heels of his master, and all he gets out of the carnage in which his blood dyed the whole earth is a new set of heels to grind into his exploited bones and a fresh and lusty vampire to drain his life-blood.

Away with all such perfidious doctrines; forever away with such a vicious subterfuge and treacherous betrayal!

The people *are* ready for their day. *THE PEOPLE,* I say. Yes, *the people!*

Who are the people? The people are the working class, the lower class, the robbed, the oppressed, the impoverished, the great majority of the earth. They and those who sympathize with them are THE PEOPLE, and they who exploit the working class, and the mercenaries and menials who aid and abet the exploiters, are the enemies of the people.

That is the attitude of Lenin and Trotsky in Russia and was of Liebknecht and Rosa Luxemburg in Germany, and this accounts for the flood of falsehood and calumny which poured upon the heads of the brave leaders and their revolutionary movement from the filthy mouthpieces of the robber regime of criminal capitalism throughout the world.

The rise of the working-class is the red spectre in the bourgeois horizon. The red cock shall never crow. Anything but that! The Kaiser himself will be pitied and forgiven if he will but roll his eyes heavenward, proclaim the menace of Bolshevism, and appeal to humanity to rise in its wrath and stamp out this curse to civilization.

And still the "curse" continues to spread—like a raging conflagration it leaps from shore to shore. The reign of capitalism and militarism has made of all peoples inflammable material. They are ripe and ready for the change, the great change which means the rise and triumph of the workers, the end of exploitation, of war and plunder, and the emancipation of the race. Let it come! Let us all help its coming and pave the way for it by organizing the workers industrially and politically to conquer capitalism and usher in the day of the people.

In Russia and Germany our valiant comrades are leading the proletarian revolution, which knows no race, no color, no sex, and no boundary lines. They are setting the heroic example for worldwide emulation. Let us, like them, scorn and repudiate the cowardly compromisers within our own ranks, challenge and defy the robber-class power, and fight it out on that line to victory or death!

From the crown of my head to the soles of my feet I am Bolshevik, and proud of it.

"The Day of the People has arrived!"

The Class Struggle, February, 1919.

"Preacher sheriff" hangs victim

FROM PULPIT TO THE GALLOWS

The other day a Christian clergyman, fittingly named Robb, officiating as a Christian sheriff, murdered an alleged Christian murderer named Weeks by springing a trap that dislocated his neck and left him hanging in mid-air till he was dead, in the Christian penitentiary in the Christian city of Fort Madison, under the Christian law of the Christian State of Iowa, in the Christian United States of America.

The man Weeks who was killed in the name of the Christian law by the Christian clergyman-sheriff Robb, vehemently protested his innocence with his last breath.

And here is what the pious and conscientious barbarian who killed him in the name of the law had to say in answer to his victim's piteous plea:

"In the eyes of God and man, I am doing my duty. I would pull that lever even if I felt in my heart that this man was innocent of the crime for which he was dying."

There is not a doubt that this Christian sheriff who graduated from the pulpit to the gallows, and who has the conscience of a cobra and the heart of a hyena, would have said and done the same monstrous thing if the victim of his Christian piety had been his own brother.

There is presented in this clergyman-sheriff, this theological hangman, this unblushing Christian savage, a rare specimen for biological analysis. His heart, if he has one, would no doubt reveal the arrested development of a jackal under microscopic examination.

On the eve of the barbarous execution the Christian hangman was interviewed by a staff correspondent of the *Chicago Herald and Examiner* and I quote from his report as follows:

"A few minutes before Robb had fulfilled his duties as minister by shriving the man he executed. Even as he pulled the scaffold lever Weeks protested his own innocence and pronounced Robb a murderer. As the preacher-sheriff walked up to the scaffold he carried in his mind the hysterical pleadings of a sobbing wife that he resign as sheriff rather than act as executioner, while in his pockets were dozens of letters and telegrams telling him that if he pulled the lever he would be sending himself to hell.

" 'It is my duty to execute this man,' he told the writer as he walked into the penitentiary. 'All the tears in the world, all the protests in the world could not shake me from doing what I consider my duty to my God and my fellow men.' "

The gruesome picture of the monster here presented that would make an ape shudder, is not yet complete. The account proceeds:

"At 11:55 a. m. Robb called the witnesses and went to the scaffold. He led Weeks out, and the prisoner addressed the newspaper men.

" 'I am innocent,' he said. 'They are making me die for something another man did. The man who kills me is a murderer.'

"He looked directly at Robb, but the latter returned the stare unmoved.

"Some day,' said the prisoner, 'he will be punished.'

" 'It is noon, the time has come,' said Robb, and led Weeks up the scaffold runway.

"The parson-sheriff adjusted the noose without a word.

" 'It is too far in front,' said Weeks, and Robb changed the knot.

"The executioner turned to the big iron lever. His jaw tightened perceptibly. His slouch hat was pulled down over his eyes.

" 'I am innocent,' came in muffled words from Weeks.

"With a tremendous jerk Robb sent the lever over and the body fell.

"Silently Robb turned and walked down the scaffold, but when he saw Weeks' feet touching the ground he went back and held the body up by the rope for fully two minutes while the scaffold was fixed.

"Robb, 33, was chaplain of the 168th Iowa Infantry in France."

After reading this, unless a man has the hyena-heart of Robb, he blushes scarlet with shame for his species and feels like following the example of Jean Meslier, the French priest who, when he was about to die, got down on his knees and begged Almighty to forgive him for having been a Christian.

The real tragedy of the monstrous affair is the conscientious Christian (?) scruple with which the horrible legal crime was committed.

Robb believed in his heartless soul that he was doing his Christian duty to God and his fellow man.

The bloodthirsty Jehovah of the ancient Jews and the satanic Mosaic law have illuminating illustration and vindication here.

Robb's conception of God as a monster of ferocity leaves nothing to the imagination in picturing the devil.

For a deed of refined torture, of downright savagery, of atrocious cruelty and inhumanity, look to the pious barbarian with a theological training and professing God. The robed beasts in the Coliseum of Rome who shrieked with laughter, roared with merriment and howled with delight while other beasts were tearing innocent heretics and slaves into bloody shreds, were of that fiendish type, and so were those pious devils of the Inquisition who solemnly folded their priestly robes about them, lifting up their bloodless faces and rolling their cruel eyes heavenward, as they unctuously chanted their refrain to the mad, unearthly screams of agony of the victims of their inquisitorial ferocity who were having their tongues torn from their throats and their joints ripped from their bodies.

After all, Robb simply incarnates in his role as Christian hangman the Christian state and nation of which he is the bloody executioner.

A nation that believes in capital punishment, in killing a human being to satisfy the law, in committing in cold blood the monstrous crime of murder in the name of justice, is simply a nation of barbarians, and if such a nation calls itself a Christian nation, the shame is all the deeper and blacker by adding hypocrisy to the atrocious crime.

If the American people can contemplate with indifference and composure the indescribably shocking spectacle of the Christian hanging of the poor wretch at Fort Madison, protesting his innocence "with muffled voice"—a spectacle that outrages all decency and disgraces all Christendom—then with all our vaunted civilization, all our professed culture, all our schools and churches, we are still in the primitive moral state of the beasts of the jungle.

It is worthy of note that Robb the hangman received his training in a theological seminary in the army. Both are reflected in his barbarous achievement—and so is his love of God in the murder of his fellow man.

The army chaplain is one of the interesting by-products of war. He is a shining example of Christian patriotism—praying for war, shouting for war, thirsting for blood and "ministering" to the soldier boy with his legs shot off, being careful always to keep his own legs out of the shrapnel zone.

How many army chaplains were killed in the late world war? There was an army of them, but if any had their eyes shot out I have not heard of them.

The Christian army chaplain prays to his Christian God to bless and prosper the killing business on his side of the line, and to have no mercy on his Christian brothers on the other side, whose Christian army chaplain is praying to the same Christian God at the same time to bless and prosper them in the same infernal business.

What cruel mockery, what ghastly hypocrisy, what idiotic superstition, and what monstrous blasphemy!

But of course war made by the ruling class, proclaimed by its politicians, must be blessed by its priests.

Every preacher in Christendom howled for the world war and shrieked for blood with now and then a rare exception who was driven from his pulpit in disgrace if not sent to the penitentiary to expiate his crime.

How many of these rampant warriors of the cloth, these pious followers of the lowly and gentle Jesus who turned their pulpits into filthy sties of the profiteering pirates and screamed for war and blood— how many of these Christian clergymen who betrayed the Prince of Peace they profess to worship, had their own legs torn off, their own eyes gouged out, their own bowels ripped from their bodies?

How many one-armed, one-legged, sightless, shell-shocked army chaplains answer to the roll call?

Sheriff Robb, the Christian army chaplain who officiated at the Fort Madison murder, true to his degenerate breed, took no chances on the battlefields of France of being deprived of giving his state the benefit and reflecting the glory of his army education and experience.

Why, I wonder, do they not have prizefight chaplains and bullfight chaplains to bless the gruesome game and pray for the defeat of the other side?

New York Call Magazine, October 29, 1922.

Woman—comrade and equal

The "London Saturday Review" in a recent issue brutally said: "Man's superiority is shown by his ability to keep woman in subjection." Such a sentiment is enough to kindle the wrath of every man who loves his wife or reveres his mother. It is the voice of the wilderness, the snarl of the primitive. Measured by that standard, every tyrant has been a hero, and brutality is at once the acme of perfection and the glory of man.

Real men do not utter such sentiments. He who does so prostitutes his powers and links himself once more to the chattering ape that wrenches the neck of the cowering female, glorying as he does so in the brute force that is his.

Yet the sentiment is not confined to a moral degenerate, who writes lies for pay, or to sycophants who sell their souls for the crumbs that arrogant wealth doles out to its vassals. It is embodied and embedded in the cruel system under which we live, the criminal system which grinds children to profits in the mills, which in the sweatshops saps women of their power to mother a race of decent men, which traps the innocent and true-hearted, making them worse than slaves in worse than all that has been said of hell. It finds expression in premiers hiding from petticoated agitators, in presidents ignoring the pleading of the mother of men, in the clubbing and jailing of suffragettes; in Wall Street gamblers and brigands cackling from their piles of loot at the demands of justice. It is expressed in laws which rank mothers and daughters as idiots and criminals. It writes, beside the declaration that men should rebel against taxation without representation, that women must submit to taxation without representation. It makes property the god that men worship, and says that woman shall have no property rights. Instead of that, she herself is counted as property, living by sufferance of the man who doles out the pittance that she uses.

Woman is the slave of a slave, and is reckoned fit only for companionship in lust. The hands and breasts that nursed all men to life are scorned as the forgetful brute proclaims his superior strength and plumes himself that he can subjugate the one who made him what he is, and would have made him better had customs and institutions permitted.

How differently is woman regarded by the truly wise and the

really great! Paolo Lombroso, one of the deepest students of mind that time has ripened, says of her:

"The most simple, most frivolous and thoughtless woman hides at the bottom of her soul a spark of heroism, which neither she herself nor anybody else suspects, which she never shows if her life runs its normal course, but which springs into evidence and manifests itself by actions of devotion and self-sacrifice, if fate strikes her or those whom she loves. Then she does not wince, she does not complain nor give way to useless despair, but rushes into the breach. The woman who hesitates to put her feet into cold, placid water throws herself into the perils of the roaring, surging maelstrom."

Sardou, the analytical novelist, declares:

"I consider women superior to men in almost everything. They possess intuitive faculty to an extraordinary degree, and may almost always be trusted to do the right thing in the right place. They are full of noble instincts, and, though heavily handicapped by fate, come well out of every ordeal. You have only to turn to history to learn the truth of what I say."

Lester F. Ward, the economist, the subtle student of affairs, gives this testimony:

"We have no conception of the real amount of talent or of genius possessed by woman. It is probably not greatly inferior to that of man even now, and a few generations of enlightened opinion on the subject, if shared by both sexes, would perhaps show that the difference is qualitative only."

I am glad to align myself with a party that declares for absolute equality between the sexes. Anything less than this is too narrow for twentieth-century civilization, and too small for a man who has a right conception of manhood.

Let us grant that woman has not reached the full height which she might attain—when I think of her devotion to duty, her tender ministries, her gentle spirit that in the clash and struggle of passion has made her the savior of the world, the thought, so far from making me decry womanhood, gives me the vision of a race so superior as to cause me to wonder at its glory and beauty ineffable.

Man has not reached his best. He never will reach his best until he walks the upward way side by side with woman. Plato was right in his fancy that man and woman are merely halves of humanity, each requiring the qualities of the other in order to attain the highest character. Shakespeare understood it when he made his noblest women strong as men and his best men tender as women.

Under our brutal forms of existence, beating womanhood to dust, we have raged in passion for the individual woman, for use only. Some day we shall develop the social passion for womanhood, and then the gross will disappear in service and justice and companionship. Then we shall lift woman from the mire where our fists have struck her, and set her by our side as our comrade and equal and that will be love indeed.

Man's superiority will be shown, not in the fact that he has enslaved his wife, but in that he has made her free.

Pamphlet published by the Chicago Socialist Party, Ill., undated.

Sacco and Vanzetti

AN APPEAL TO AMERICAN LABOR

The supreme court of Massachusetts has spoken at last and Bartolomeo Vanzetti and Nicolo Sacco, two of the bravest and best scouts that ever served the labor movement, must go to the electric chair.

The decision of this capitalist judicial tribunal is not surprising. It accords perfectly with the tragical farce and the farcical tragedy of the entire trial of these two absolutely innocent and shamefully persecuted working men.

The evidence at the trial in which they were charged with a murder they had no more to do with committing than I had, would have convicted no one but a "foreign labor agitator" in the hydrophobic madness of the world war. In any other case the perjured and flagrantly made-to-order testimony, repeatedly exposed and well known to the court, would have resulted in instantaneous acquittal. Not even a sheep-killing dog but only a "vicious foreign-radical" could have been convicted under such shameless evidence.

Sacco and Vanzetti were framed and doomed from the start. Not all the testimony that could have been piled up to establish their innocence beyond a question of doubt could have saved them in that court. The trial judge was set and immovable. It was so ordained by the capitalist powers that be, and it had to come. And there must be no new trial granted lest the satanic perjury of the testimony and the utter rottenness of the proceedings appear to notoriously rank and revolting in spite of the conspiracy of the press to keep the public in ignorance of the disgraceful and damning facts.

Aside from the disgustingly farcical nature of the trial which could and should have ended in fifteen minutes in that master-class court, the refined malice and barbaric cruelty of these capitalist tribunals, high and low, may be read in the insufferable torture inflicted through six long, agonizing years upon their imprisoned and helpless victims.

It would have been merciful to the last degree in comparison had they been boiled in oil, burned at the stake, or had every joint been torn from their bodies on the wheel when they were first seized as prey to glut the vengeance of slave drivers, who wax fat and savage in child labor and who never forgive an "agitator" who is too rigidly honest to be bribed, too courageous to be intimidated, and too defiant to be suppressed.

And that is precisely why the mill-owning, labor-sweating malefactors of Massachusetts had Sacco and Vanzetti framed, pounced upon, thrown into a dungeon, and sentenced to be murdered by their judicial and other official underlings.

I appeal to the working men and women of America to think of these two loyal comrades, these two honest, clean-hearted brothers of ours, in this fateful hour in which they stand face to face with their bitter and ignominious doom.

The capitalist courts of Massachusetts have had them on the rack day and night, devouring the flesh of their bodies and torturing their souls for six long years to finally deal the last vicious, heartless blow, aimed to send them to their graves as red-handed felons and murderers.

Would that it were in my power to make that trial judge and those cold-blooded gowns in the higher court suffer for just one day the agonizing torture, the pitiless misery, the relentless cruelty they have inflicted in their stony-hearted "judicial calmness and serenity" upon Sacco and Vanzetti through six endless years!

Perhaps some day these solemn and begowned servants of the ruling powers may have to atone for their revolting crime against innocence in the name of justice!

They have pronounced the doom of their long-suffering victims

---

and the press declares that the last word has been spoken. I deny it.

There is yet another voice yet to be heard and that is the voice of an outraged working class. It is for labor now to speak and for the labor movement to announce its decision, and that decision is and must be, SACCO AND VANZETTI ARE INNOCENT AND SHALL NOT DIE!

To allow these two intrepid proletarian leaders to perish as red-handed criminals would forever disgrace the cause of labor in the United States. The countless children of generations yet to come would blush for their sires and grandsires and never forgive their cowardice and poltroonery.

It cannot be possible, and I shall not think it possible, that the American workers will desert, betray and deliver to their executioner two men who have stood as staunchly true, as unflinchingly loyal in the cause of labor as have Sacco and Vanzetti, whose doom has been pronounced by the implacable enemies of the working class.

Now is the time for all labor to be aroused and to rally as one vast host to vindicate its assailed honor, to assert its self-respect, and to issue its demand that in spite of the capitalist-controlled courts of Massachusetts honest and innocent workingmen whose only crime is their innocence of crime and their loyalty to labor, shall not be murdered by the official hirelings of the corporate powers that rule and tyrannize over the state.

It does not matter what the occupation of the worker may be, what he is in theory or belief, what union or party he belongs to, this is the supreme cause of us all and the call comes to each one of us and to all of us to unite from coast to coast in every state and throughout the whole country to protest in thunder tones against the consummation of that foul and damning crime against labor in the once proud state of Massachusetts.

A thousand protest meetings should be called at once and ring with denunciation of the impending crime.

A million letters of indignant resentment should roll in on the governor of Massachusetts and upon members of the House of Representatives and the Senate of the United States.

It is this, and this alone, that will save Sacco and Vanzetti. We cannot ignore this duty to ourselves, to our martyr comrades, to our cause, to justice and humanity without being guilty of treason to our own manhood and outraging our own souls.

AROUSE YE TOILING MILLIONS OF THE NATION AND SWEAR BY ALL YOU HOLD SACRED IN THE CAUSE OF LABOR AND IN THE CAUSE OF TRUTH AND JUSTICE AND ALL THINGS OF GOOD REPORT, THAT SACCO AND VANZETTI, YOUR BROTHERS AND MINE, INNOCENT AS WE ARE, SHALL NOT BE FOULLY MURDERED TO GLUT THE VENGEANCE OF A GANG OF PLUTOCRATIC SLAVE DRIVERS!

Labor Defender, July, 1926.

The negro workers

Friends and Comrades and Fellow-workers—I feel especially complimented by the invitation which has made it possible for me to stand in this inspiring presence tonight. I must first of all thank you and each of you in all sincerity for this very cordial greeting—this hearty manifestation of your sympathy and goodwill for the cause for which I am to speak to you tonight, and for the all too generous introduction of my young Comrade, the Chairman of the occasion, which touches me too deeply for words. I return my thanks to the dear little children whose floral offerings so enrich and reward me for the little that I have been able to do in the service of this great cause. The one regret of my life is that I have so little to give in return for all that is given me.

This great movement which I have been trying to serve; this movement in the interest of a higher social order, a nobler humanity, a diviner civilization that has given me my principles and my ideals and the right to live and serve—I am only sorry that it is in my power to give so little in return.

I am more than glad to see the colored people represented here tonight. From the beginning of my life my heart has been with them. I never could understand why they were denied any right or any privilege or liberty that the white man had a right to enjoy. I never knew of any distinction on account of the color of the flesh of a human being. Indeed, when I think of what the colored people have been made to suffer at the hands of their supposedly superior race, every time I look a colored brother in the face I blush for the crimes that my race has committed against his race. (Great applause.)

I do not speak to my colored friends tonight in any patronising sense; I meet them upon a common basis of equality; they are my brothers and my sisters, and I want nothing that is denied them, and if there is one of them who will shine my shoes and I am not willing to shine his, he is my moral superior. (Applause.) One reason why I became a Socialist was because I was opposed to this cruel discrimination against human beings on account of the color of their skin. I never could understand it. When I traveled over the Southern States thirty-five years ago organizing the workers, oh, what a desolate, unpromising situation it was! I made my appeal to them wherever I went, to open their doors to the colored workers upon equal terms with the white workers, but they refused. Poor as most of them were, they still felt themselves superior to the colored people.

It is one of the surest indications of their own ignorance and their own inferiority (applause); but, of course, they are not conscious of it. There is what they call a race prejudice, that is simply another name for ignorance (applause), and you can trace it to that and that alone. It is comparatively easy to forgive a man who has wronged you, but it is a very difficult thing to forgive the man that you have wronged. And this is the attitude in which we find our colored brother who has been the victim of this so-called civilization during the last two centuries; and if there is any man who has read the history of the institution of chattel slavery on American soil, from its beginning— from its inception through all of its frightful stages, and who does not blush for himself and for his Anglo-Saxon race, it is because he is something less than a real human being. (Applause.)

Stolen from their native land, torn from their families ruthlessly by the brutal hand of conquest, and then thrown aboard vessels and herded like animals, half of them perishing on the way over from starvation or disease or ill-treatment, and the rest put upon auction blocks and sold to the highest or lowest bidders, and then through the years that followed designedly kept in ignorance and then despised, persecuted and punished because of their alleged inferiority!

The colored man has just as much in him that is potential and capable of development as the white man (great applause); and all he needs is a chance, that is all; he has never had that chance. (Renewed applause.)

I am sometimes surprised to think of the claims that are made in the name of religion and the much-vaunted Christian civilization that has everything in it but Christianity. (Applause.) Even in the great Christian Church the colored people have got to sit aloft—(A Voice: "Next to Heaven." Laughter.)—and I have had many a heated argument down in the Southern States and sometimes narrowly avoided trouble, making the contention that the colored man was a human being and had some rights that the white man ought to respect. (Applause.)

I remember on one occasion down in Atlanta, we had a Labor meeting and they had a loft to which the colored people were admitted. It was so far aloft that I could hardly see them (laughter) and I wondered if they could hear me; but they did, because their ears were attuned to a voice that had some promise for them. (Applause.) And I noted in the course of my address that I received no applause from below; it all came from the loft. (Laughter.) I paused long enough to say "the intelligence of this audience is in the gallery" (laughter and applause); and if they had had intelligence enough to understand what I said, I might have been lynched that night. (Laughter.)

On another occasion down at Montgomery, Alabama, where I was to speak at the Opera House, they had the line sharply drawn and said no colored people should be admitted. It so happened that the colored people had worked most faithfully and energetically for the success of that meeting, and when they appointed a committee which came to my hotel and notified me that they were to be excluded, I said, "We will go there together, and if you excluded, so will I be excluded; if you cannot be admitted, I will not speak." (Great applause.) Well, there is one thing that the "superior" white man loves better than he hates the Negro, and that is the coin. (Laughter.) The manager had $50 coming for the use of the Opera House, and he wanted the money, and when I said I wouldn't speak unless he opened the doors to the colored people, he changed his mind very reluctantly to receive his $50. (Applause.)

When we were organizing the American Railway Union in 1893, I stood on the floor of that Convention all through its deliberations appealing to the delegates to open the door to admit the colored as well as the white man upon equal terms. They refused, and then came a strike and they expected the colored porters and waiters to stand by them. If they had only admitted these porters and waiters to membership in the American Railway Union there would have been

---

a different story of that strike, for it would certainly have had a different result.

I remember one occasion down in Louisville, Kentucky, where we were organizing and they refused to admit colored workers to the union. A strike followed—a strike ordered exclusively by the white workers. After having ignored the colored workers and refused them admission, the strike came and the colored workers walked out with the white ones. Notwithstanding they had been excluded and insulted, they went out, and the strike had not lasted long until the white men went back to work and broke the strike, leaving the colored men out in the cold in spite of their loyalty to the white workers.

I have a word to you workers—you colored workers—about your duty in this campaign—your duty to yourselves, your families, your class and to humanity. I am not here asking for anything for myself. If I were seeking office, you know, I would not be in the Socialist Party. (Applause and laughter.) I want to speak to you very plainly tonight, especially you colored people, and have you understand that it is not in my power to do anything for you but to take my place side by side with you. That is all I can do. (Applause.) But while I can do nothing for you there is nothing that you cannot do for yourselves. (Applause.) There is one thing that I want to impress upon your minds tonight; it is self-respect. You can compel the respect of others only when you respect yourselves. (Applause.) As long as you are willing to be the menials and servants and slaves of the white people, that is what you will be. (Applause.) You have to realize that there are 12,000,000 of you in this nation, and that if you will unite and stand together and be true to each other, you will develop a power that will command respect. (Applause.) As long as you are unorganized—as long as you are indifferent, as long as you are satisfied to remain in ignorance you will invite contempt and receive it, but when you rise in the majesty of your manhood and womanhood, close up the ranks and stand together, you will command respect and consideration and you will receive it. (Thunderous applause.) It is the only way you ever will receive it. Everything depends upon your education. You have a brain; you can develop your capacity for clear-thinking. That is a duty owing to yourselves and your class, to your race and to humanity. (Applause.) That is the appeal I am making to you tonight.

Haven't you been long enough in the service of the capitalist parties to realize that they have no earthly use for you save only as they can perpetuate their system and keep you in servitude? The Republican party has trafficked in you, lo, these many years; the party that is unspeakably corrupt but still claims a monopoly of Abraham Lincoln and brazenly calls itself the party of Lincoln—what use have they for you? There was a time in my life, before I became a Socialist—when I was still young and had the vanity of youth and the ambition and enthusiasm of a boy—when I permitted myself as a member of the Democratic party to be elected to a State Legislature. I have been trying to live it down. (Laughter.) I am as much ashamed of that as I am proud of having gone to jail. (Applause and laughter.)

There is a peculiar fatality that seems to hang over me. Every time I am nominated as a candidate for the President by the Socialists, the capitalists send me to jail or to the penitentiary. (Laughter.) Some paper said: "Debs started for the White House and got as far as Atlanta." (Laughter.)

I was, as I have said, a member of a Legislature. I used to meet with the politicians—Republicans as well as the Democrats; I became familiar with their political methods; I heard them over and over say in campaigning: "Now, we have got to figure on how to handle the "Nigger" vote; how much does it amount to and what will it take?" Well, a thousand colored voters are worth about one job on the police force or a mail carrier; if there are only about 500, why, a cleaning job at the courthouse. That is about all they have ever given you and all they ever will give you. They do not associate with you; they have nothing in common with you. They want you segregated. When a race riot of any description comes, they are always armed against you. You know what they have done for you in the last thirty years in the way of recognizing you decently as human beings and giving you an equal chance with other human beings to work out your destiny.

Now, if you still persist—you colored people—in remaining in either the Republican or the Democratic party, you are stultifying yourselves; you are insulting your race; you are barring the door in your own faces—the door that leads to emancipation. The time has come for you to realize what your position is in these capitalist parties. They are both alike. I challenge anybody anywhere to show me the slightest difference between them from the working man's point of view.

I am speaking for the workers tonight. It does not make any difference to me where they were born or what the color of their skin may be, or what their religion is, or their creed, or anything of that kind. I ask no question as to that; they are all of the working class, the lower class, the class that does all of society's useful work, that produces all its wealth, and makes all the sacrifices of health and limb and life through all the hours of the day and night; the class without which the whole social fabric would collapse in an instant. It is this class regardless of color that creates and supports all civilization; this class that in all the ages of the past, throughout history, in every nation on earth has been the lower class; for the badge of Labor has always been the symbol of servitude and upon the brow of Labor there has always been the brand of social inferiority.

In the ancient world your ancestors were slaves, owned by their masters, whipped by their masters, put to death by their masters the same as other domestic animals. In the Middle Ages for a thousand years the serfs were not allowed to own an inch of soil; they could work only on condition that they produced for the benefit of the idle, aristocratic lord and baron who owned the land and who rioted in the luxury wrung from their sweat and misery. They also fought for him to enlarge his domain believing in their ignorance it was their patriotic duty to fight and die for the sovereign baron who looked down upon them with contempt. You are no longer the slave or the serf, but you are the wage earner in the present capitalist system. Your interests are all identical; you do all the useful, productive work but you do not work for yourselves; you have no legal right to work; you can work only if you are permitted to work by the owners of the tools with which you work. You made the tools and use the tools; but they own them and they might almost as well own you; for as long as you work with their tools, what you produce belongs to them; they become fabulously rich producing nothing while you remain poor producing everything. And this applies to white and black alike.

The race question as we come to understand it, resolves itself into a class question. At bottom it is a class question. The capitalist cares no more about the white worker than about the black worker. What he wants is labor power—cheap labor power; he does not care whether it is wrapped up in a white skin or a black skin.

Has he one bit more consideration for the white slave than he has for the black slave? No, not at all; they are all the same to him regardless of color; they are all in the working class; they are his legitimate prey. He owns the natural resources; he owns the tools; they have got to produce for him.

Under chattel slavery, the colored man seized with the aspiration to be free, ran away from his master. You do not run away from yours; when you run it is not away from but toward the factory whistle; you are afraid you won't get there soon enough. You work for your master and he becomes rich, and he does not know you; and why should he? He belongs to the upper class; you are in the lower class. He is useless and that is why he is in the upper class. (Laughter and applause.) Parasites all go to the top; they all float on the surface.

But now comes an election! That is the season of the year when their politicians come before you white and black workers. They do not discriminate against you colored people then. On the contrary they are glad to look into your intelligent faces and tell you that the beads of honest sweat that glisten on your manly brow are more precious than the jewels that blaze and flash in the coronet of a queen. (Laughter.) That is the one kind of jewelry—the one monopoly you absolutely control. They tell you that they are so greatly impressed by your intelligence and so proud to stand in your presence. But after the election is over they fold up their tents and like the Arab, they silently fade away. They do not associate with you; you do not belong to the same clubs they do. You do not play golf with them on their links; you don't wear the same kind of clothes they do nor live in the same houses, nor eat the same kind of food. No; they are in a class of their own, notwithstanding you are all supposed to be absolutely equal before the law.

This is capitalism under which an insignificant minority of our people own and control the Nation's industries—all the sources and means of our common life. They would if they could own the sunlight and have a meter on every sunbeam. They have taken possession of about everything else. You are at their mercy. When you work it is by their consent; when you work it is for them; when you work it is primarily to produce profit for them; not to enable you to support your wife and children; that is purely incidental.

Under this system you workers white and black are scarcely above the animal plane. You work and produce like the silkworm; like the coral insect that builds islands and continents and perishes as it builds; and when you die you leave no trace behind that you were ever upon earth.

You are not hired to think but to work. That is why they call you "hands." You will hear them say: "I work a hundred hands"; I work fifty "Niggers." Black "hands"; white "hands"; all "hands" (laughter); not men but "hands." The capitalist calls you his "hands"; he himself is not a hand; he is a head; he lives in a palace and you are his "hands"; and the "hands" vote on election day to perpetuate the system under which he is at the top and they at the bottom; and that is why the "hands" are told that this is the greatest country on the face of the earth—the one country in which all enjoy equal liberty.

The time has come for you to open your eyes and to stand erect and to realize that you have a head as well as hands; that you can think as well as work; and if you will but unite and think and act in accordance with your intelligence, you need no longer to deform your hands in the interest of the parasites that hold you in contempt. They are an insignificant minority and yet they rule in every department of this Government, and they rule through your ignorance, and the Socialist is frank enough to tell you that you are ignorant and that you may become intelligent.

We do not flatter you and call you intelligent to keep you ignorant. We would have you understand that your masters rule because of your ignorance, because you still insist upon remaining in the Republican party or the Democratic party—and they are equally corrupt, only more so; both are financed from the same source, and our Comrade Chairman quite aptly quoted Sinclair, the oil king, in confessing to the United States Senate Committee investigating his deals that he contributes to both Republican and Democratic campaign funds. And why should he not? They are both his parties; both stand for his system; for the private ownership of this nation's industries; for the exploitation of the working class; for wage-slavery, and if that is what you want, stay with them; they will fulfill that program to your heart's content.

But have you not within you the holy spark of freedom, the glowing aspiration to be a man?—**not a slave but a MAN!** You must know what that is—a being with a soul that throbs with a desire and aspiration to know life. The working class does not know life. They are absorbed in maintaining an existence and that is not life; and while they are engaged in the endless struggle that taxes their energies, devitalizes and ages them prematurely, wears them out and casts them on the scrap-heap, they are not living. They are not permitted to know what life is in its larger, nobler and diviner meaning. They are never thrilled with those higher and holier emotions that put them in touch with all that lifts up and elevates men and women until they can, from the loftiest altitudes, sing to the stars. They do not know what music is. And the capitalists themselves are not very much better off. How wholly undeveloped they are in that higher intellectual, moral and spiritual sense! I have met many of them. I have been amazed at their ignorance. They are shrewd, to be sure; they are cunning; they can instinctively see an opening for profit; oh, they have a marvelous faculty for seeing a chance to skin somebody, and especially each other. (Laughter.) They belong to the same church; they go to the same prayer meeting but when they approach the edge of a "business" transaction, oh, how keenly they eye each other; not because they do not know each other, but because they do. Each is a good Christian and each is trying to avoid just what he is trying to do to the other. (Applause.)

Take them just as you find them; put them on this stand tonight; ask them a few questions about the history of their own country and you will be appalled by their ignorance. Point out to them a magnificent painting on canvass that breathes and throbs with genius; they have little or no capacity for its appreciation. Point out to them a great plumed monarch of the forest; the kind you can put your arms about it and hear its mighty heart throb; the kind that dominates the forest by its majesty and inspired Joyce Kilmer's beautiful poetic homage. You remember Joyce Kilmer—put to death, murdered in the late war; one of the fine poetic souls slaughtered and sacrificed on the altar of Mammon. It was he who wrote: "A tree that in the spring may wear, a nest of robins in its hair. Poems are made by fools like me, but only God can make a tree!" And you point out that a towering and venerable tree to the fully developed capitalist and he regards it soberly for a moment and then draws forth his lead pencil and figures out how many feet of commercial lumber there are in that proposition. (Laughter.)

I wish I had time enough—but I have not—to trace American history from the days of the Revolution when the "Fathers" made their monumental mistake by the compromising with chattel slavery. Had they but taken the advice of Thomas Paine (applause) the Civil War would not have resulted; that terrible sacrifice would have been averted. Thomas Paine protested and wrote the first article ever written in this country against chattel slavery just as he wrote the first article ever written in this country in favor of woman's rights—the same heroic Thomas Paine whose religious beliefs in "The Age of Reason" that followed completely isolated him from all intelligent understanding, from all human sympathy, and he is not yet forgiven for having had the courage to be true to himself and to the best he knew. Thomas Paine inspired the Declaration of Independence that Thomas Jefferson wrote. (Applause.)

You call Washington today the "father of his country." And yet in his day he was denounced as a "notorious outlaw." (Applause.) The "father of his country" was the owner of chattel slaves as were the rest of the "fathers." They thought that perfectly consistent with that period; it does not detract from their historic achievement.

I can understand why the Tory press—the press of the then ruling class—charged Washington with being a common thief for confiscating their property. He was literally despised by them when he unsheathed his sword to fight for independence.

Thomas Jefferson was denounced as a vicious incendiary, Sam Adams as a disreputable agitator and Patrick Henry—you know what they said of him. (Applause.) I stood not long ago upon the spot where he stood when he hurled his immortal challenge in the face of the Government and exclaimed: "Give me liberty or give me death"; and I fancied I heard the hisses of the aristocrats that thronged the gallery who despised and denounced him as a traitor to his country. What was the state of his country at that time? A great majority of the colonists in their ignorance believed that God had anointed a king from on high to rule over them, and to question the divine authority of that king was treason, and he who was guilty must be punished without mercy. That was the blind stupidity of the great majority. Here let it be observed that the minorities have made the history of this world. The popular and reactionary majorities have perished in oblivion in their own ignorance.

In every age there have been a few men and women with new ideas—ideas in conflict with the established order of things. The class in power have always insisted upon perpetuating that power; they want no change; they combat every idea that suggests a change; they want to feel secure in "the established order of things."

In every age there have been a few men and women with moral courage, who stood erect and defied the storms of hatred and detraction. After a time—after they had been persecuted, vilified and imprisoned—after they had been burned at the stake and their ashes scattered to the winds by the hands of hate—the slow-moving world finally caught up to where they stood and fought for humanity and then it paused long enough to weave garlands for their graves and erect monuments where they sleep.

There were only a few of the American revolutionary leaders; only a few; and they stood face to face with a gainsaying populace who protested: "We believe in the king and we must be loyal to the king." They did not believe that the people had capacity for self-government; they were too weak, too helpless and dependent, and God had to provide them with a king to rule over them. That is what they believed. There were only a few who said: "We do not need a king; we can govern ourselves"; and they persisted in their odious agitation until they finally aroused the colonists and then came the war and the king was overthrown; the divine right to rule was trampled under foot with contempt; the foundations of the Republic were laid, the immortal Declaration was issued, and for the first time in history, politically speaking, men stood forth clothed to a limited extent with sovereignty.

How many of you are aware of the fact that the first drop of blood shed in that revolutionary struggle was that of a Negro? Crispus Attucks, to whom Boston has now erected a monument, was the first to be shot down by the British soldiers in the Boston massacre. (Applause.) And he was a Negro—the man whose blood was first to be shed for American independence; but you do not read that in the school histories. (Applause.) The Negro gets no credit for that martyrdom.

If there is any institution in the history of the world, the recollection of which should turn the cheek of humanity crimson with shame, it is the infamous institution of chattel slavery in the United States. (Applause.) There is no parallel to it in sheer, stark brutality in all the history of the world. You have never been given the facts; you never will be by the standard historians—they who represent the interests of the ruling class who subsidize and support them. You will never get that history until it is written by the working class itself. And some day it will be written. Some time American history will be reviewed. You never hear much about the people in history. You read about the exploits of the murderous military chieftains. All history glorifies them, but about the common people—the people who alone make history, how little reference is made to them! McMaster made a departure in his history and for the first time you now read about the lives of the common people in American history. Hitherto their achievements have not been deemed of sufficient importance to place upon record.

We come down to the final development of the institution of chattel slavery which culminated in the terrible war. The great majority, of course, upheld that brutal institution. And likewise the politicians and statesmen (so-called), the editors and the preachers—oh, how many there were who solemnly opened their Bibles and quoted passages to show that slavery had been ordained of God himself and that it was wicked to oppose it! Of the few heroic souls who declared it a crime Elijah Lovejoy was one of the first, and appealed to me in my earliest boyhood. I think I can almost hear him even now: "I have sworn eternal opposition to slavery and by the help of God, I will not turn back." And then they murdered him! Garrison followed and then Wendell Phillips (applause); and the great towering, commanding intellectual and moral figure in that fierce struggle was Wendell Phillips. (Applause.) He saw it most clearly of all, faced it most courageously of all, and never once faltered in his devotion to the colored race. (Applause.) After chattel slavery had been abolished Garrison believed that the struggle was over—but he was mistaken—Wendell Phillips knew better, and some estrangement resulted on that account.

Wendell Phillips, with discerning and prophetic vision, said: "This is the prelude—just the prelude to the far greater struggle—the struggle that will involve not only the black slaves but all the slaves of the earth in the mightly movement for their common emancipation. That is what Wendell Phillips said and he wrote the first Socialist platform ever written in the United States. Read the platform he wrote as far back as 1871 and see how uncompromisingly he faced the situation. They threatened him with the vengeance of the mob but he did not falter, he never wavered.

Wendell Phillips was a most wonderful combination of head and heart, soul and conscience (applause), and when the real truth is known about his commanding part in that historic struggle, the colored people will know that the real champion they had from first to last was Wendell Phillips. (Great applause.)

I am not unmindful of the heroic part that William Lloyd Garrison took, or Theodore Parker, or Gerrit Smith who was driven insane by their brutal persecution; or Susan B. Anthony or Elizabeth Cady Stanton or Maria Childs, or any of those magnificent women who were in the forefront espousing the cause of their sex and at the same time the cause of the disfranchised Negro; who faced insult and persecution through many years. I have them all in mind and from my heart I pay the humble tribute of my gratitude and my admiration and love to them all.

But the greatest hero of them all was John Brown. (Thunderous applause.) I have taken time enough to go to Charlestown and to Harper's Ferry, and I have walked in his footsteps all the way from the old engine house where he made his heroic stand until he gave up his noble life on the gallows—every step of the way. And I thought of his wondrous courage and consecration and of the majesty, the spiritual loftiness of a human being who could give up his life as freely as he did for a lowly and despised race that could not understand him. There were members of that race so subservient to the masters in their ignorance that they begged for the privilege of braining him while he was in prison; but they only excited his compassion because he knew it was due to the very institution of chattel slavery that they had been sunk to that bestial moral state.

John Brown, when the crisis came, stood forth almost alone and struck the blow—the immortal blow that put an end to that most infamous of human institutions. Victor Hugo from across the Atlantic protested: "Think of a republic murdering a liberator," when they were about to put him to death; and after they had executed him for his heroism and his humanitarianism, Victor Hugo said: "The time will come when you Americans will realize that your John Brown was a greater liberator than your George Washington." (Applause.)

I appreciate all these heros and martyrs, including Lincoln who was vilified like no other American statesman ever was by that cruel and relentless power that organized the Ku Klux Klan after the war, and which is now seeking to revive that fanatical institution for the persecution of the negro.

I am on the colored man's side as against all those that are attempting to keep him in servitude. (Applause.) And I am glad that the colored people are exercising self-restraint and facing this persecution with intelligence, which is commanding more and more respect.

Let the Ku Klux spend its force. It consists of the self-appointed custodians of American liberty; but just let them alone; give them time and they will soon enough complete their round and close up their record. (Applause.)

I honor and appreciate all those who stood forth through the revolutionary conflict—through the struggle against chattel slavery—all who served and sacrificed to make it possible for me to stand on this platform tonight and to enjoy some degree of liberty and progress. I thank them all, and the only way I can repay them is by doing, as they did for me, what I can for those who are to come after us. And that is why I am here tonight.

I want to make my modest contribution to this campaign of education and organization that gives you the opportunity to register your protest against capitalist corruption and misrule as well as the degree of your class consciousness and intelligence. (Applause.)

A matter of local interest to you in this campaign is the housing proposition. The law expires in February coming. It will not be re-enacted by the old parties. All the combined landlords have launched a campaign of opposition to it. This is an issue in which the workers are especially concerned. The rich are not worried about housing conditions. It is the workers who will be the prey of the greedy landlords of New York. That is an important issue in this campaign and the Socialist Party stands squarely for the re-enactment of the housing law and for the curbing of capitalistic greed in the interest of better housing conditions for the benefit of the working class and the exploited and suffering poor. (Applause.)

There is another matter of local interest. I was waited on today at my hotel by a delegation of policemen and City firemen. When officers of the law call on me they usually have a warrant (laughter); but on this occasion they were on a perfectly friendly mission.

When we had our meeting at Brooklyn the other night they had half the police force of that section there, just as they had at Toledo, the police surrounding the Opera House. But Socialist meetings are uniformly orderly. (Applause.) You never hear of a disorderly Socialist meeting. We appeal to the intelligence of the people (applause); we seek to educate them. A Socialist meeting has something of a religious spirit in it.

But they sent the police force there because they said "he is a very dangerous man; there is no telling what may happen when he comes to town." (Laughter.) You see they are afraid of a man who tells the truth (applause); that is the one thing they cannot stand. (Applause.) And if you cannot be bribed or brow-beaten—if you cannot be intimidated, if you insist upon being true to your own soul's integrity, and speak what is in your heart, then of course, you must expect to pay the penalty, and I have been and am now ready to pay to the limit. I went down to Atlanta for three years almost; that was my fifth term in one of the peculiar educational institutions of capitalism and it has all had its good results. (Laughter.) But I have no bitterness; I have no resentment. I felt sorry for the man who had to lock me up. He did not want to do it.

Soon after I was in prison I came in touch with a colored man who had a most tragic history. He had been there for thirty years and ten years of that he had been placed in solitary confinement because they couldn't break his spirit. When they insulted him he resented it and defended himself. When I got down there I heard about him. His name was Sam Moore. He was one of the many, many colored men who never had a chance in life. In his childhood—in his very infancy he was tossed out into the world; he knew only poverty and neglect; his mother was dead seven years before he knew it. He was never in school; no one had ever given him a kind word; buffeted about he tried to help himself and fight his way along; he got arrested, as they all do, was put in jail, got into a quarrel and in a fight that followed he chanced to kill another prisoner when they sent him to the penitentiary, more than thirty years ago, and he has been there ever since. When I came in touch with him they said: he is a bad man." I soon found him to be a brother. The Chaplain was asked: "What has Debs done to Sam Moore, he is an entirely different man?" "The chaplain answered: "Just loves him; that's all." (Applause.) Oh, the magic and the power of human love, were it but understood! Sam Moore had never been touched by the hands of kindness; everything that was combative in his nature was developed by the cruel, inhuman treatment he had been subjected to all his life. And when I came down there and we met face to face on the same level, I said to myself, if I had been born as Sam Moore was and under the same condition, I would be Sam Moore; I would be where he is now. I am not one bit better than he. On the contrary I was reminded of the divine Easterner who prayed to his Allah: "Be Thou merciful to the vicious and forgive them; Thou has already blessed the virtuous by

---

The negro workers 199

making them so."

As I thought of Sam Moore and of the environment and conditions under which he had been reared and had to suffer and struggle, I made allowance accordingly, and he was the last inmate I saw when I left that prison.

There were almost three thousand human beings there. The prison is the poor man's institution; the rich don't go there, no matter what crime they may commit. About one-third of the prisoners were colored people, and they used to come to me when they had petitions to make or there was some little service I could render them. I used to write their letters and I could not but sympathize with them. They tried to segregate them in the prison. We were occasionally permitted to see moving pictures. They admitted the white men to one side of the auditorium and the colored men to the other side. Some of the white "superior" element said: "Let the Niggers sit in the rear"; and so on the next occasion they allowed the white men to occupy all the front seats and put the colored men in the rear where they hardly see the stage. They appointed a committee to call on me to see what they could do about it. I said "I am with you; we will protest against the injustice." We did and we put an end to it. After that the colored men were given the same consideration as the white prisoners.

I loved all of those almost three thousand prisoners, charged with every conceivable offense against society. I treated them all as if they had been members of my own family, and there was not one of them I would not have invited to my table or to my home. They were poor, most of them ignorant; they never had a fair chance. They had, for the most part, committed some petty offense and were pushed into the penitentiary and branded as "convicts."

The lowest thing about a prison is often the prison guard—the only fellow I was ashamed to associate with. (Laughter.) The last inmate I saw when I left prison was Sam Moore. There was a fine woman in that neighborhood whose sympathy had been enlisted, and on the day I left she brought a beautiful cake she had baked. She said: "This is for Sam," and the warden said: "I will send it to him"; I said: "No, please send for Sam, I wish to place it in his hands and bid him good-bye." Sam came. There was something of the majesty of the man about him, notwithstanding his thirty years of cruel usage and persecution. He was like some monarch of the forest that the tempest had riven and denuded. But he still stood erect, unbroken in spirit. I presented him with the cake and the tears rolled down his face. At parting we put our arms around each other and wept together. That was my farewell scene in the Atlanta prison. I can still hear, in broken words, the sobbing entreaty: "I want to get out of here and to be where I can do for you and your family anything in my power all the rest of my life." That was Sam Moore, the man they had said was a desperado, an incorrigible and dangerous criminal. He was as tender and responsive as a child; the divine within him had not been extinguished; all he needed was the touch of human kindness; and that is what has been denied him and his race through all the centuries.

Give a colored man the same chance, the same opportunity that you give a white man, and he will register as high upon the mental and moral thermometer of civilization. (Great applause.) Give him a chance! And that is what the Socialist Party is going to do. (Applause.) We admit colored members to our Party upon equal terms with the rest. We sit side by side with them in our Party councils. They are welcomed gladly to all our conferences and conventions. We treat them in no patronizing sense. We are not doing them any favor. They are our comrades and our equals, and we want them to have every right and privilege we enjoy.

I wish to speak a final word for the policemen and firemen. When they came to see me today and stated their mission, I declared myself in favor of their referendum. It is with this referendum they propose to establish a wage minimum of $2,500. The policemen and firemen are in the working class—all of them; and we are with them in their efforts to secure a living wage. (Applause.) You sometimes think these policemen, when they seek to "protect society against the Socialists," are hostile to us. When we were at Brooklyn, as I passed through their serried ranks they whispered to me: "We are with you." (Applause.) One of them said: "It will not do for the Ku Klux to try to do anything to you here tonight." (Laughter.) They are trying to get $2,500 a year and they are entitled to it; considering the cost of living $2,500 with a family to support is a small enough income. We are with them and we hope you will all join in their effort to secure a living wage for themselves and their families. (Applause.)

I want to say a word for the "Messenger" and to commend the high ability of its editorial management. I read it with especial pride and satisfaction. It is a high grade publication. It is a true champion

---

The negro workers 201

of the colored workers and every one of you ought to give it your encouragement and support.

I appeal directly to you colored workers. You have got to build up your own press; you have got to develop your own power; you will never count until you do. Unite with all other workers in the unions; unite with them in the Socialist Party; develop your industrial power and your political power. Most of you are inclined to buy the capitalist newspapers and support the capitalist press and every time there is a strike you know what side they are on. You will never hear the truth until you hear it through your own press.

Then there is the daily "Leader," a Labor paper published in New York. The "Leader" ought to have the support of the workers. We have got to build up a press of our own. It is vitally important because everything depends upon education.

It is a tremendous struggle. It is going to take time and what most people call sacrifice. There is no sacrifice, however, so far as I am concerned, because what I can give the cause I give with joy and it comes back to me in riches untold. I have made no sacrifice for Socialism. I would sacrifice only if I refused the privilege of serving it. I would sacrifice only if I violated my conscience and failed to give myself to this struggle with every atom of my energy and every drop of my blood. And with what joy! It keeps me young and vigorous and alive in action. It is a privilege and not a sacrifice to go to jail for the cause. (Applause.) How gladly I would spend the rest of my days there if need be, or go to the gallows, or anywhere in the service of Socialism! (Great applause.)

You and I and all of us are alike interested in the present campaign. You hear the same "argument" on the part of the old politicians you have heard here in New York for over forty years. I am not personally interested in their vilification of each other—their mutual charges and accusations. Take their word for it and they are all grafters and thieves. They say so and they certainly know each other for they have been in close affiliation for a long time. If you are going to cast your vote for either of these corrupt capitalist parties and if you are going to give your support to those candidates who are committed to keep you in servitude how can you look yourselves in the face on the day following election without a blush of shame?

Sever your relations with these capitalist parties that are of the past. They disgrace the memory of Jefferson and Lincoln. Sever your relations with them and join this new party, this party of the future, especially you young people. It is vain to appeal to some of the older ones; they are petrified; they have long since ceased to think; they are led; they belong to the Republican party because their father did, or to the Democratic party because their grandfather did. Everything since their grandfather lived has changed except their grandsons. (Laughter.) If you have the spirit of the future; if you have the aspirations to be men and women; if you are capable of thinking for yourselves, stand up for just once and see how long a shadow you can cast in the sunlight; take an inventory of your mental and moral resources and ask yourselves in sober earnest: "What can we do for ourselves, and for our class, and for humanity"? Think!! You have never done that in the past. You have the capacity to see, to think, to understand, and to take your place in this great modern crusade, the greatest in all history.

Everywhere the awakening workers are lifting their bowed bodies from the earth—these toiling and producing masses who have been the mudsills of society through all the ages past. They are learning at last how to stand erect and hold up their heads and press forward toward the dawn, keeping step to the inspiring heartthrobs of the impending Social revolution. They are of all races; they are of all colors, all creeds, all nationalities. They have made a great beginning in Russia. (Applause.) The Soviet Republic has stood for five years against the combined capitalisms of the world; vilified and misrepresented shamefully, but they still hold the fort. The reason we do not recognize their Republic is because for the first time in history they have set up a Government of the working class; and if that experiment succeeds, good-bye to capitalism throughout the world! (Applause.) That is why our capitalist Government does not recognize Soviet Russia. We were not too proud to recognize the Czar nor to have intercourse with Russia whilst Siberia was in existence and human beings were treated like wild beasts; when women were put under the lash and sent to Siberia and brutalized and dehumanized. We could calmly contemplate all this and our President could send congratulations on his birthday to the imperial Czar of Russia. We could then have perfect intercourse with that Government, but we are now so sensitive under our present high standard of moral ethics that we cannot recognize Soviet Russia. But the time will come when the United States will recognize the

Soviet Republic of the Russian people.

Meanwhile we will wait, watch and work. We will improve our minds and develop our capacity to think and act together. We shall get closer and closer in touch day by day, increasing the store of our knowledge, dispelling the darkness of ignorance, and moving steadily toward the light.

You and I and all of us are comrades; we are brothers and sisters. Let us get into perfect unity with each other and stand upon one common basis of equality with the high aspiration to emancipate ourselves from the degrading thraldoms of past ages. Let us as workers organize industrially so that we may be fitted to take control of industry. We will then relieve the Rockefellers, the Garys and the Sinclairs of their sinacure jobs; we will give them an opportunity to make an honest living for the first time in their lives. (Applause.) We will take full possession of industry. Every man and woman will have the inalienable right to work with the most improved machinery. The machine will be the only slave—no body to starve, no back to scar, no heart to break, no soul to crush. The machine will work for us and we shall then have leisure time enough to cultivate the graces of life; to know and love and serve each other, and to begin the march to the first real civilization the world has ever known. The liberating hour is soon to strike—and if you are true to yourselves you can speed the day of its coming. Triumphant International Socialism will then proclaim the emancipation of the working class and the brotherhood of all mankind. At last that inspiring vision of Ingersoll will have been realized:

"I can see a world where thrones have crumbled and where kings are dust. The aristocracy of idleness has perished from the earth. I can see a world without a slave; man at last is free. Nature's forces have by science been enslaved. Lightning and light, wind and wave, frost and flame and all the secret, subtle forces of earth and air are the tireless toilers for the human race. I can see a world at peace, adorned with every form of art, with music's myriad voices thrilled while lips are rich with words of love and truth. A world in which no exile sighs, no prisoner mourns—upon which the shadow of the cruel gallows no longer falls. I can see a world where Labor reaps its full reward and work and worth go hand in hand. I can see a race without disease of flesh or brain, shapely and fair, the married harmony of form and function, and as I look, life lengthens, joy deepens, love canopies the earth, while over all in the great dome there shines the eternal star of hope."

And in that crowning hour men and women can walk the highlands side by side and enjoy the enrapturing vision of a land without a master, a land without a slave; a land radiant and resplendent in the perfect triumph of the brotherhood of all mankind.

And now from my heart I thank you for the patience and the kindly interest with which you have listened to me. I thank you for having been here tonight and for giving me the privilege of appearing upon the platform with these comrades that I know you are going to stand by on Tuesday next—Comrade Lucille Randolph, your candidate, whom I would be so proud to vote for if I could, and Comrade Ollendorff, who incarnates the true spirit, the high principles and the lofty ideals of the Socialist movement. They are your candidates and my candidates, and if you are true to them as they have been to you, they will be triumphantly elected next week. And now good-night and a thousand thanks and good wishes! (Great and prolonged applause.)

Address delivered Tuesday, October 30th, 1923, at Commonwealth Casino, 135th Street and Madison Avenue, New York City, under the Auspices of the 21st A. D. Socialist Party of New York.